Chicago Public Library
West Pullman Branch
830 W. 119th Street
Chicago, IL 60628
312-747-1425

FORM 19

DEMCO

Extreme Origami

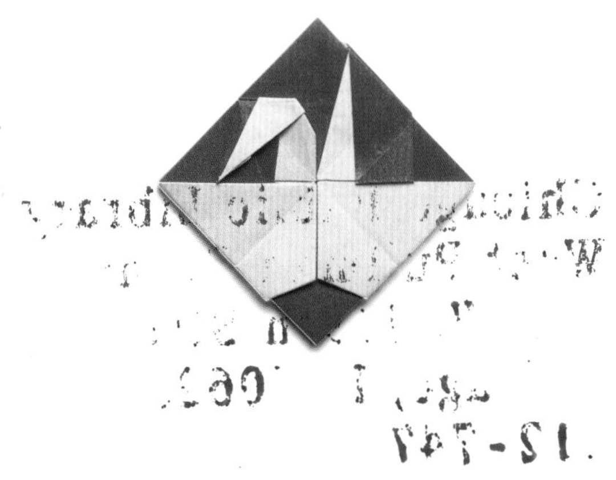

Extreme Origami

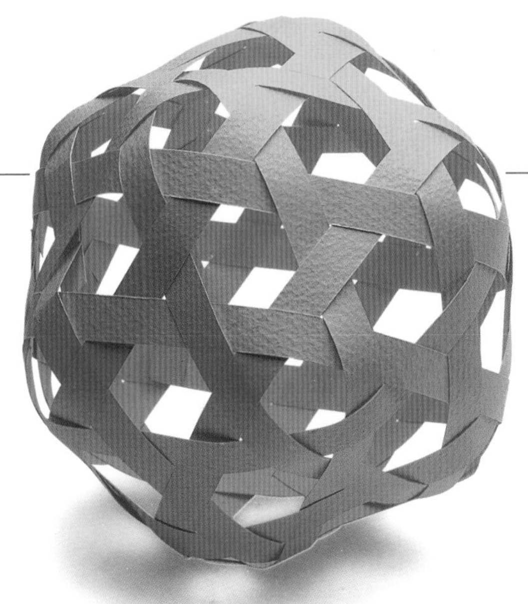

Kunihiko Kasahara

Sterling Publishing Co., Inc.
New York

Chicago Public Library
West Pullman Branch
830 W. 119th Street
Chicago, IL 60628
312-747-1425

Photography: Klaus Lipa
Layout: Kunihiko Kasahara and Michael Steihl

Library of Congress Cataloging-in-Publication Data Available

English translation by Michelle Mavigiliano and Volker Husel

Published by Sterling Publishing Company, Inc.
387 Park Avenue South, New York, N.Y. 10016
©2002 by Sterling Publishing Co., Inc.
First published in Germany and ©2001 by Augustus Verlag
in der Weltbild Ratgeber Verlage GmbH & Co. KG
under the title *Origami ohne Grenzen*
English translation ©2002 by Sterling Publishing Co., Inc.
Distributed in Canada by Sterling Publishing
c/o Canadian Manda Group, One Atlantic Avenue, Suite 105
Toronto, Ontario, Canada M6K 3E7
Distributed in Great Britain and Europe by Chris Lloyd at Orca Book Services,
Stanley House, Fleets Lane, Poole BH15 3AJ, England
Distributed in Australia by Capricorn Link (Australia) Pty Ltd.
P.O. Box 704, Windsor, NSW 2756, Australia
Printed in China
All rights reserved

Sterling ISBN 0-8069-8853-3

R07158 14924

Con

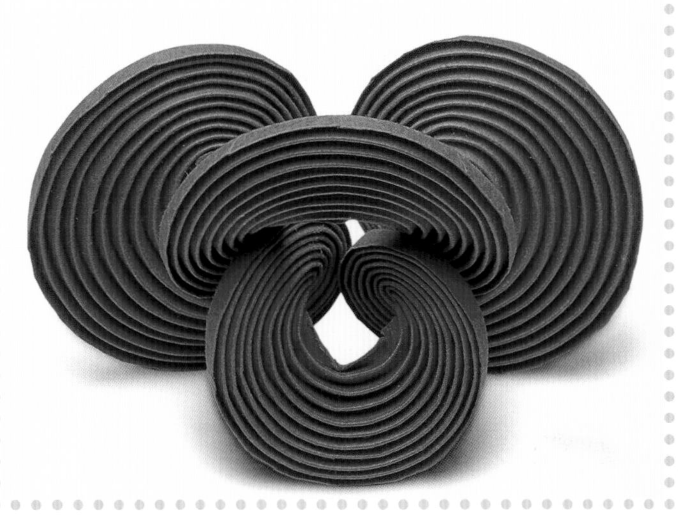

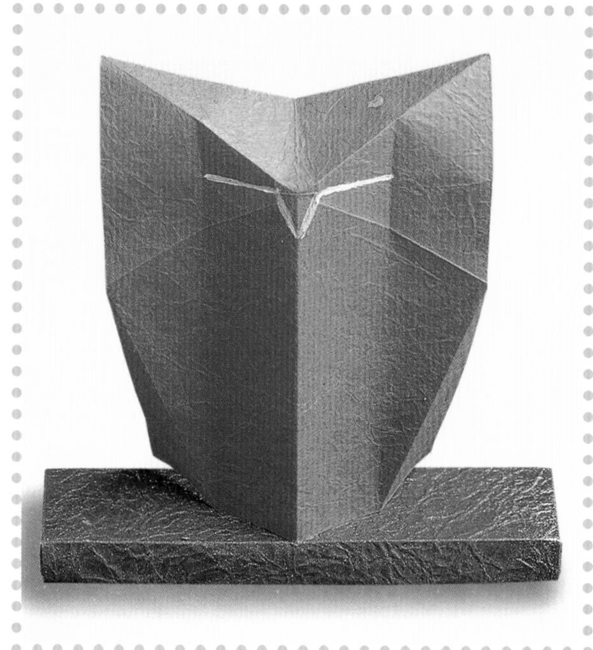

Introduction: The New Dimensions of Origami

For more than forty years I have devoted myself to origami and the geometric/mathematical design and functional principles upon which it is based. This book introduces many new possibilities with origami, which can be learned very easily.

The only requirement is that you free yourself from the traditional rules of classical origami — concerning, for example, the square paper format or the number of sheets of paper that may used. If you are able to set aside even more taboos, such as those against cutting, painting, and gluing, new horizons will begin to open in the origami heavens. The innovations are so extensive that they can be called revolutionary: new materials, new forms, and new folding and design techniques.

I was inspired to overcome the limits of origami, especially after discovering and analyzing the work of the Bauhaus School in Dessau, Germany. It was there that Joseph Albers (1888–1976), a forerunner of optical (Op) and minimalist art, taught. Among other things, Albers taught origami and paper folding in the 1920s and 1930s. His designs, in which a sheet of round paper was used to create circles, spirals, and curved shapes, immediately overwhelmed me. That was the birth of my own personal origami revolution.

I wish with all my heart that through experimentation, designing, and pushing the limits you also may experience the same fascination.

— *Kunihiko Kasahara*

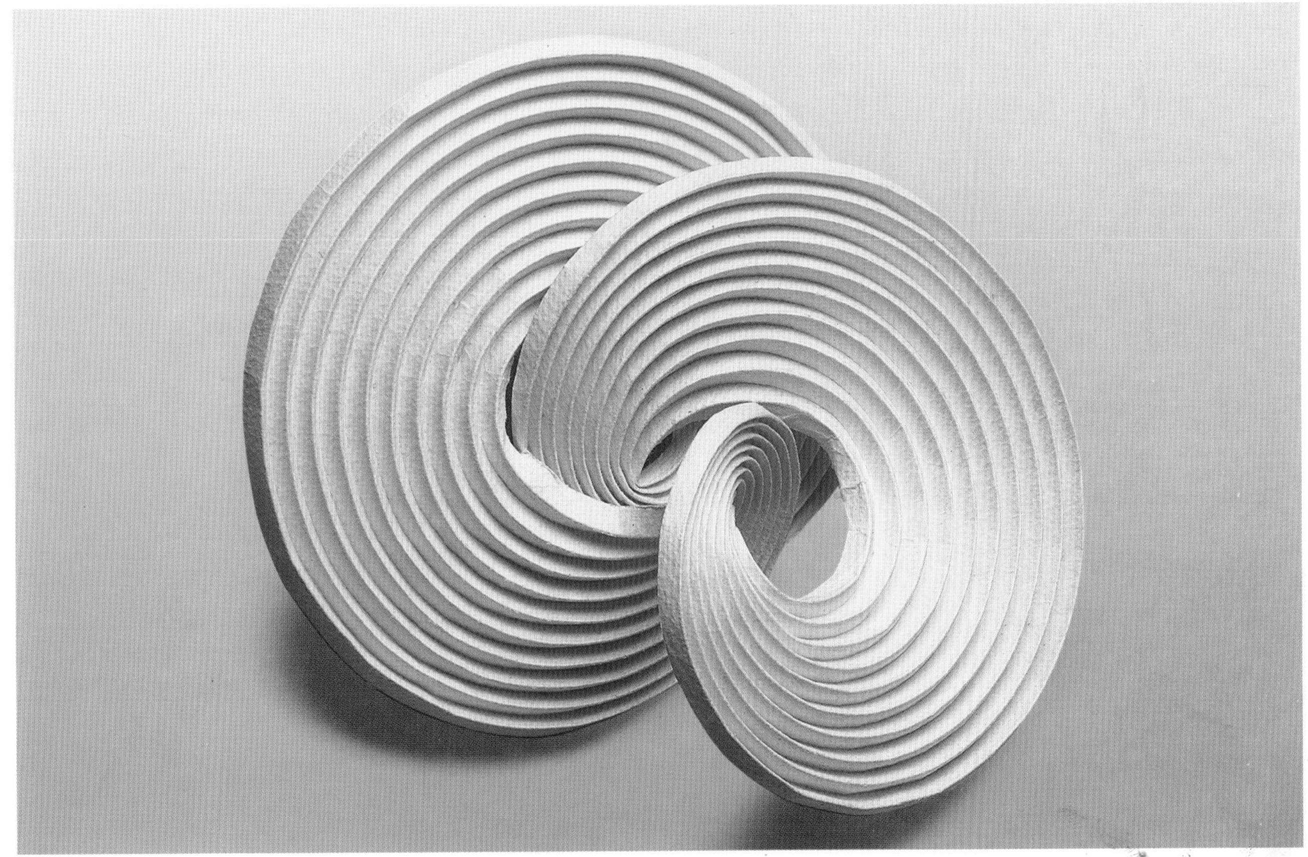

Origami Symbols

Below are the most important origami symbols. They are used all over the world and form the basis of the folding instructions in this book.

Valley fold

Mountain fold

Fold forward

Fold backward

Open, unfold, or pull out

The following drawing is an enlargement

Step fold (pleat in a mountain and valley fold like a step)

Turn the model over

Fold and unfold

Sink fold

Open and squash

Blow air into the creation

Hidden line

Cut along this line

Unequal to

Fold so one dot is over the other

> Greater than (e.g., 10 > 9)

< Less than (7 < 8)

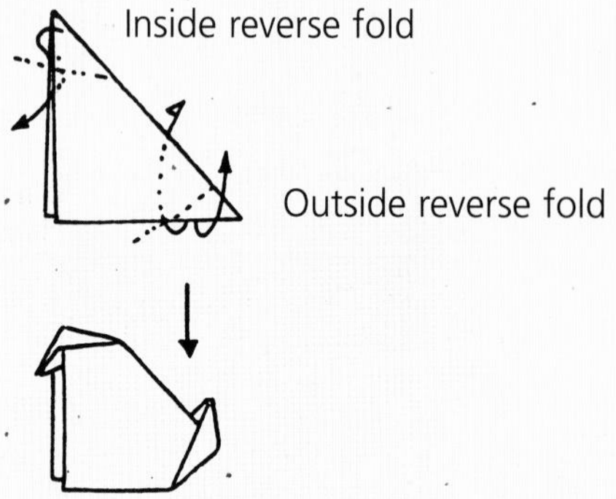

Inside reverse fold

Outside reverse fold

Chapter 1 Bent Folds and Curved Surfaces

Bent folds and curved surfaces have no place in the world of traditional origami and are sometimes termed anti-origami.

Free yourself from these restrictions to your creative freedom and be receptive to new forms that enable origami designs to become even richer and more beautiful.

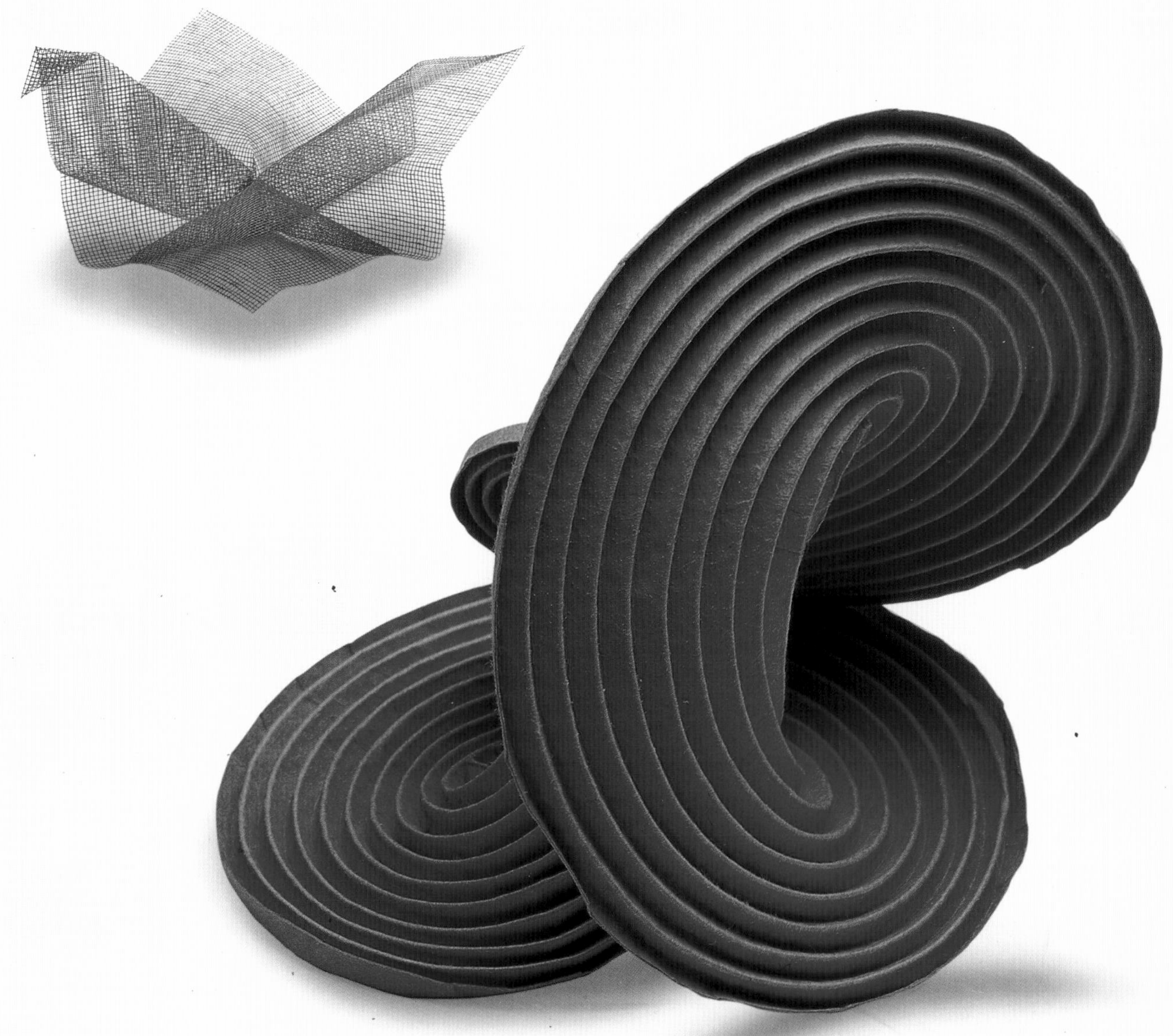

Before the Big Bang

A Picture Story

At my first meeting with Thoki Yenn, he presented me with this fantastic arching form of curves and folds, which he called Before the Big Bang. The name inspired the following picture story:

In the beginning there was neither light nor darkness, neither space nor time.

By chance, a deviation appeared.

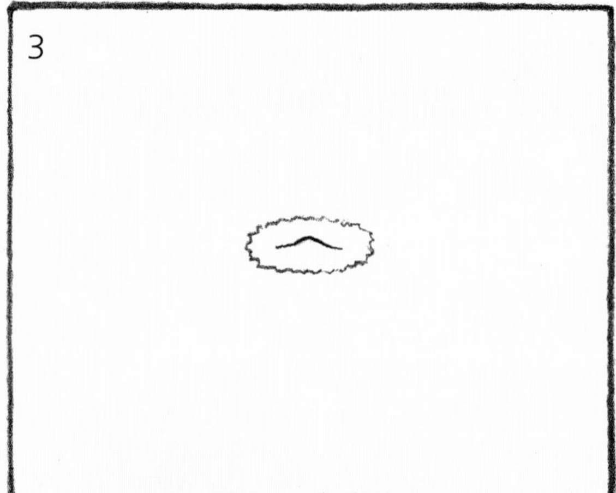

This deviation distorted the empty space.

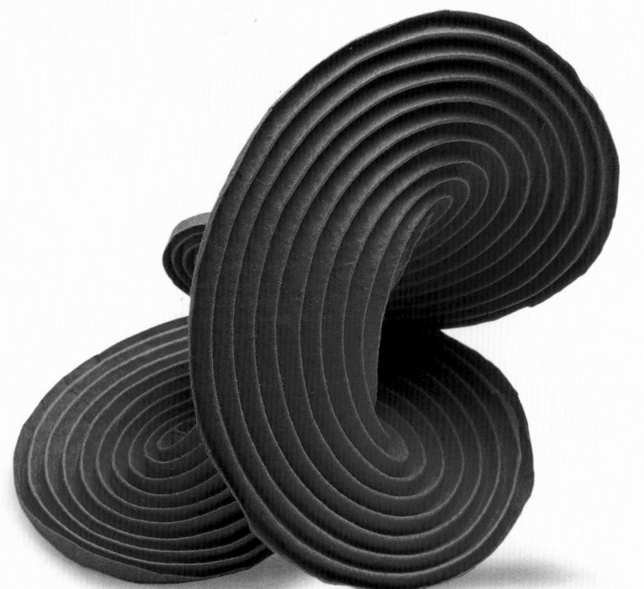

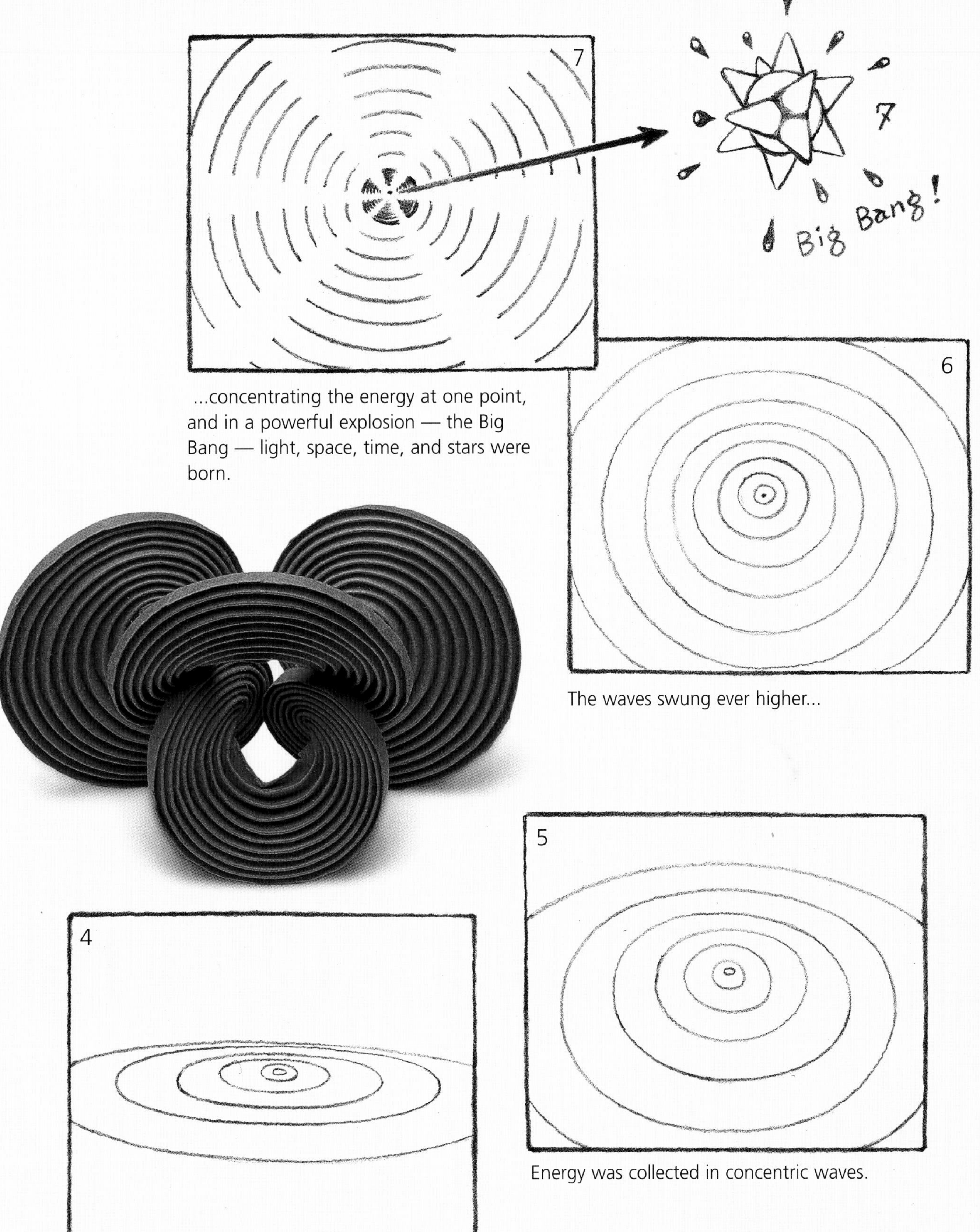

...concentrating the energy at one point, and in a powerful explosion — the Big Bang — light, space, time, and stars were born.

The waves swung ever higher...

Energy was collected in concentric waves.

The distortion spread outward in an undulating motion.

Rule 1: Using Tools

You will need some aids in creating the wonderful form on the previous page. Using tools also is taboo in traditional origami, but if one always follows that unwritten rule, there would be no exploration of new possibilities. Rule 1 of the origami revolution explains this:

Rule 1

Use every available tool that is useful to you. This means a ruler, compass, protractor, steel pen nib in pen holder, and of course a computer (nice but not necessary). It should be clearly noted that the best tools are still hands and fingers.

Creating Tools

The new dimensions of the folded shapes invented by Josef Albers and Thoki Yenn require a new type of tool.

This is what you need:

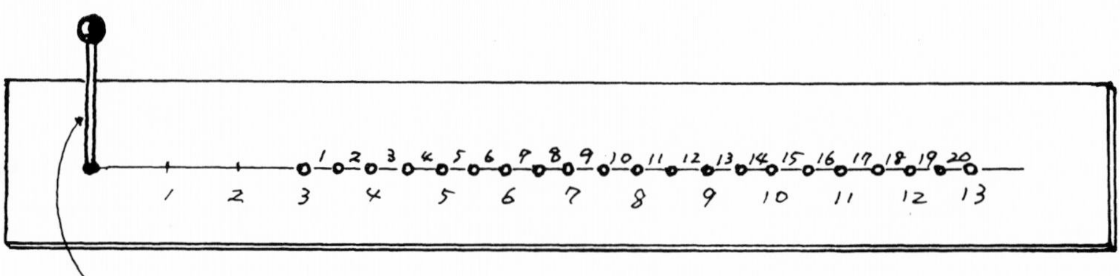

A straight pin

A homemade compass ruler made from a cardboard or plastic strip, which can be used to draw circles. To do this, you will need to punch 20 evenly spaced holes into the strip, as shown in the drawing.

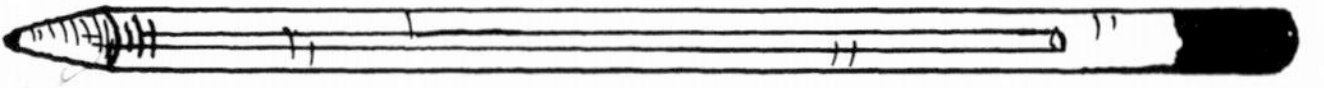

An empty ballpoint pen (no ink) or steel pen nib in a holder to score the circles on the paper.

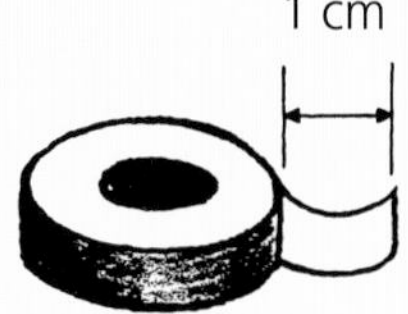

About 1 cm (1/2 inch) of tape in order to reinforce the main punch hole (see illustration on page 13)

Folding Instructions

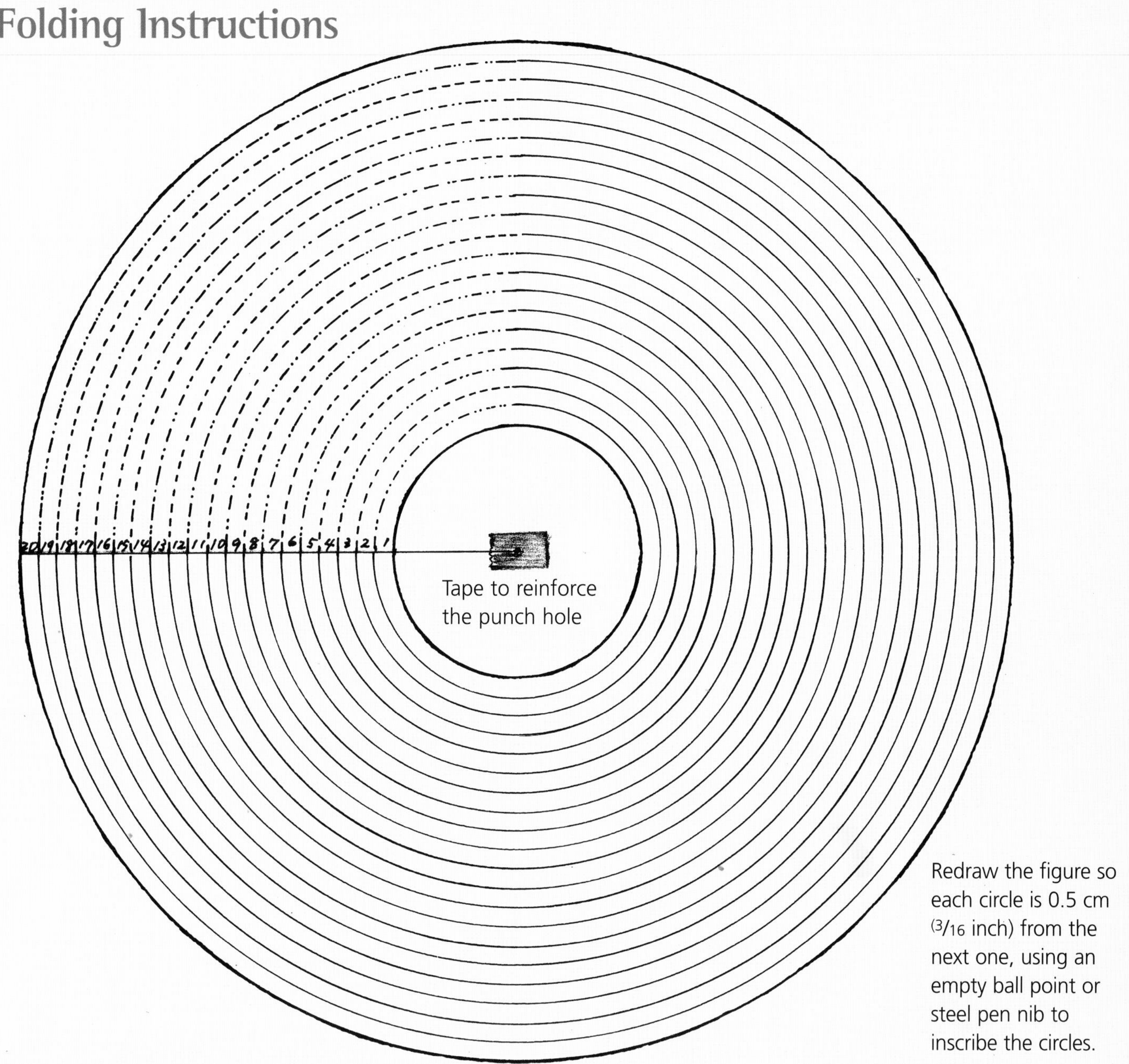

Redraw the figure so each circle is 0.5 cm (3/16 inch) from the next one, using an empty ball point or steel pen nib to inscribe the circles.

Thoki Yenn's original model of Before the Big Bang was on large paper with 26 concentric circles spaced about 1 cm (3/8 inch) apart. Here we present a smaller version which is easier to fold. Of course, if you are diligent and patient, building the model at the original size is highly recommended and well worth the effort. For our version, draw only 21 concentric circles, 0.5 cm (3/16 inch) apart. The radii of the circles are from 4.5 cm (1 3/4 inches) to 14.5 cm (5 3/4 inches).

Fasten your homemade compass ruler to the center of the paper with the pin. Inscribe each fold line into the paper by inserting the pen into a hole and turning the pen and ruler in a circle around the central point.

When inscribing the circles is complete, cut out the innermost circle of your drawing, and then cut around the largest circle to remove the drawing from the rest of the paper.

Fold on the circle lines, alternating between mountain and valley folds (see illustration above).

Variations

Before the Big Bang, the epoch-making shape by Josef Albers and Thoki Yenn, has many different faces. It is a milestone in new origami shapes. Depending on how you intertwine and configure the ring-shaped basic model (see illustration on previous page), creations with completely different appearances can be produced. And if you twist the ring to a fully extended spiral, a double helix like that of DNA is formed.

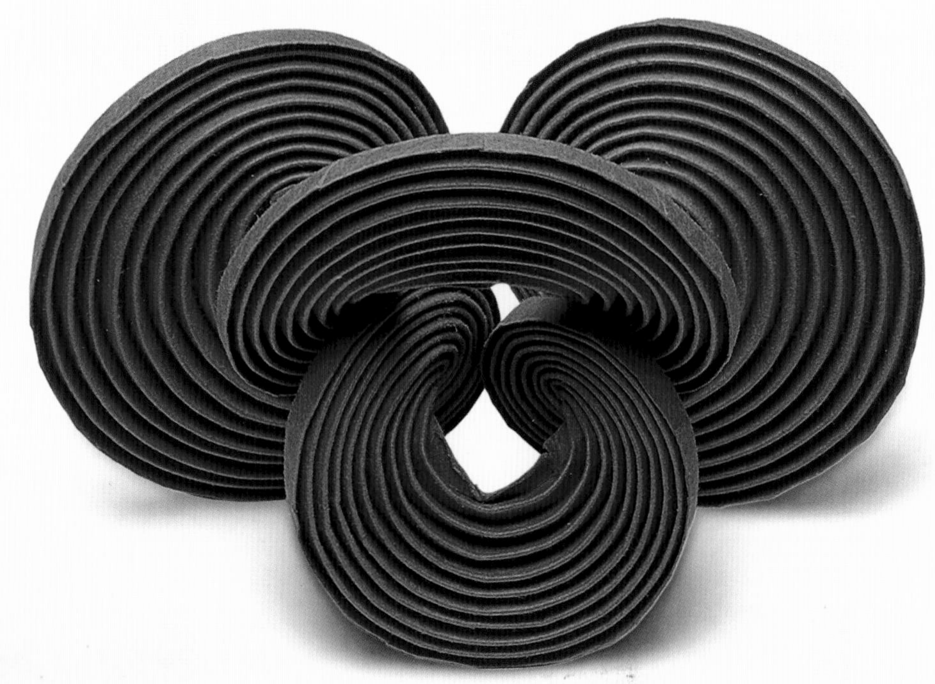

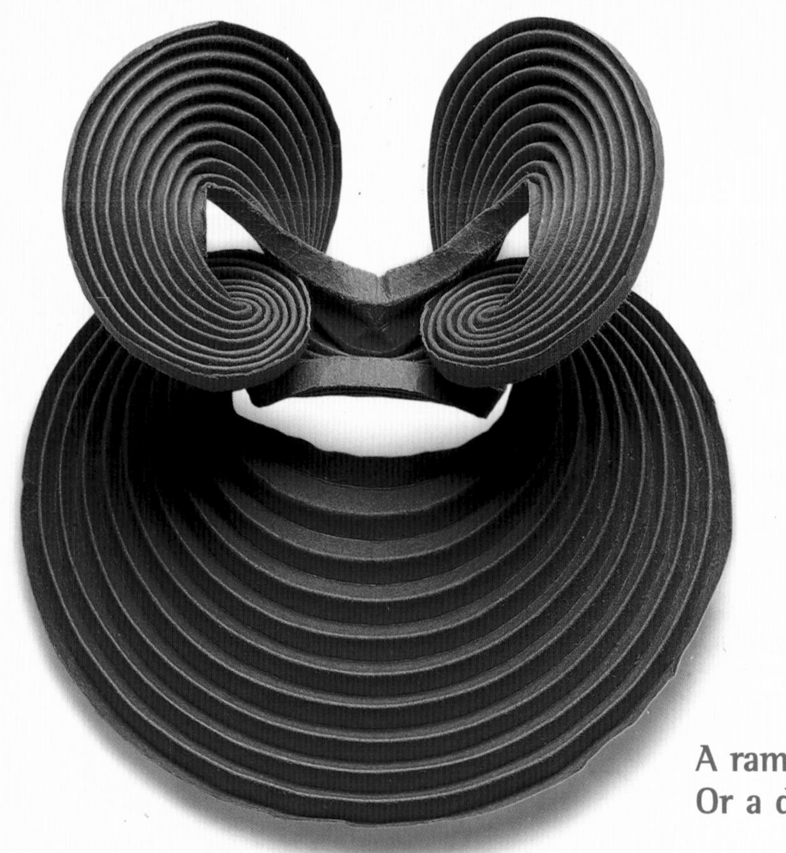

**A ram?
Or a devil?**

DNA
Double Helix

Pandanus Star

Curved surfaces are usually created from curved folds, but there are no folds used in the surface construction of the Pandanus Star, therefore the production of this form would scarcely be classified as traditional origami by many people; however, there are many good reasons for its inclusion. You will find an explanation on page 18.

The Pandanus Star is, by the way, a traditional motif in the folk art of the Okinawa Prefecture, Japan. It was originally made from the leaves of the regionally grown Pandanus shrub. In lieu of this, simple strips of paper are used here. I needed 15 years to reconstruct these nearly forgotten folding instructions.

Left: Pandanus Shrub, Iriomote Island

Below right: Pandanus fruit

Below left: Crafts made from Pandanus leaves, Taketomi Island (Folk Art Archive)

Folding Instructions

The construction is more stable with a 12.5 cm (4⅞ inch) long strip of paper. But for the moment, try to use 13 cm (5⅛ inch) strips, which make it easier to assemble.

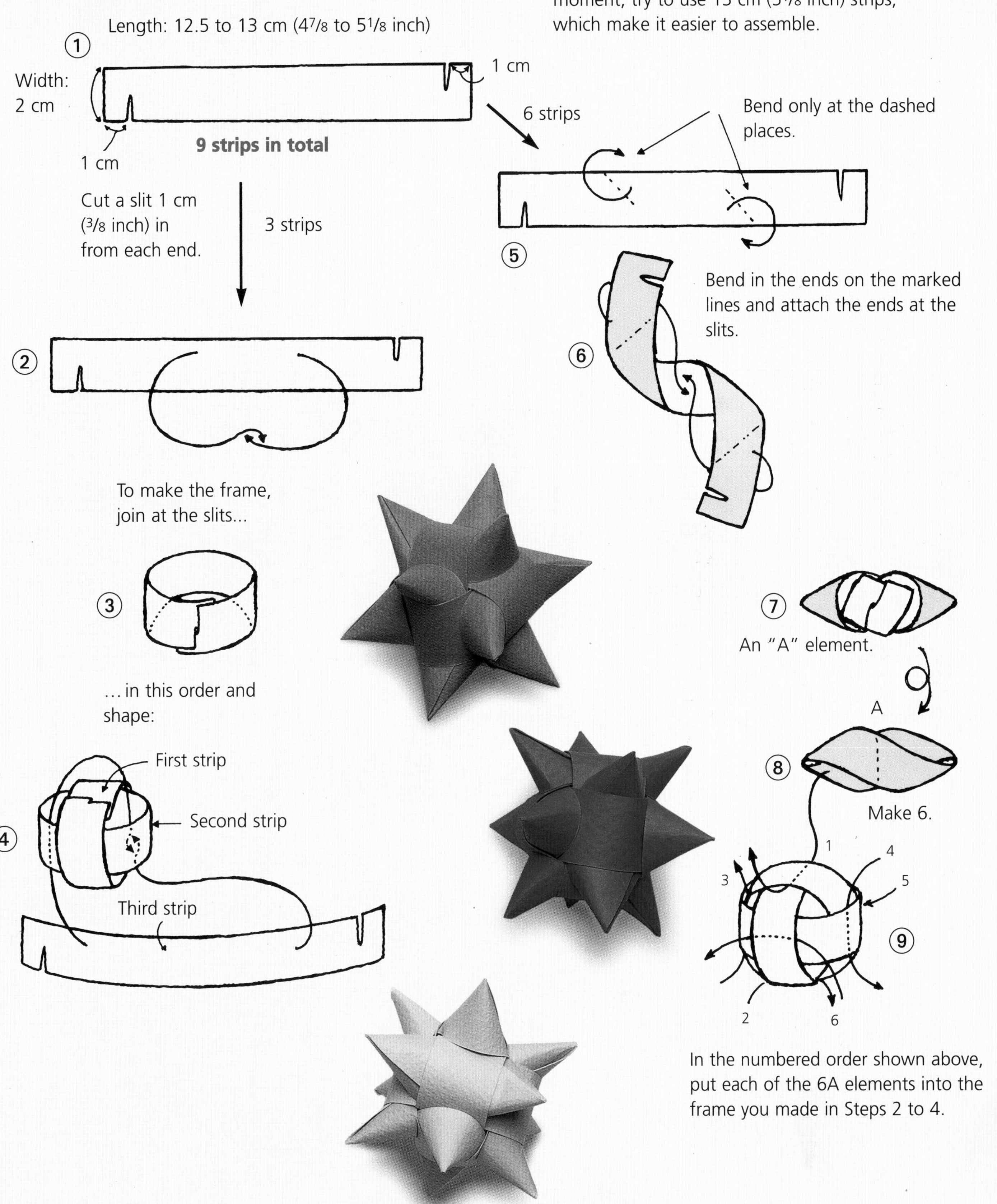

①
Length: 12.5 to 13 cm (4⅞ to 5⅛ inch)
Width: 2 cm
1 cm
1 cm
9 strips in total
Cut a slit 1 cm (⅜ inch) in from each end.
3 strips
6 strips
Bend only at the dashed places.
⑤
②
Bend in the ends on the marked lines and attach the ends at the slits.
⑥
To make the frame, join at the slits...
③
... in this order and shape:
First strip
Second strip
④
Third strip
⑦
An "A" element.
A
⑧
Make 6.
1
4
3
5
⑨
2
6

In the numbered order shown above, put each of the 6A elements into the frame you made in Steps 2 to 4.

Rules 2 and 3: Materials and Techniques

The German teacher Friedrich Wilhelm August Froebel (1782–1852), founder of the first kindergartens, realized the importance of a goal-oriented and interactive, playful education for children very early on. He appreciated origami as a teaching aid, but also incorporated different techniques and materials into his course of instruction — for example, wood, stones, nuts, textiles, and modeling clay.

From this, he developed several different activities, of which four examples are listed below:

1. Binding, plaiting, and weaving
2. Paper folding
3 Gluing and cutting paper
4. Modeling with cardboard

For the techniques in the first example, paper strips were used as a primary material, as well as ribbons and string.

This leads to Rule 2 of the origami revolution:

Rule 2

Do not limit the materials for your design to just paper! All materials that can be folded, bent, and made into strips can be used.

Finally, the third rule applies to the expansion of techniques. In this context, a linguistic phenomenon of my native language, Japanese, may be of interest: in Japanese, the words "weaving" and "folding" (both expressed by the verb *oru*) are pronounced the same way. That means that in Japanese 折り紙 paper folding 織り紙 paper weaving or おりがみ are phonetically the same.

Therefore, the Pandanus Star, a construction of curved surfaces (see page 17), would also be described as origami in Japanese.

Rule 3

In addition to folding, the traditional origami technique, other shaping methods such as plaiting and weaving should not be avoided.

The Japanese characters shown here are all pronounced "origami."

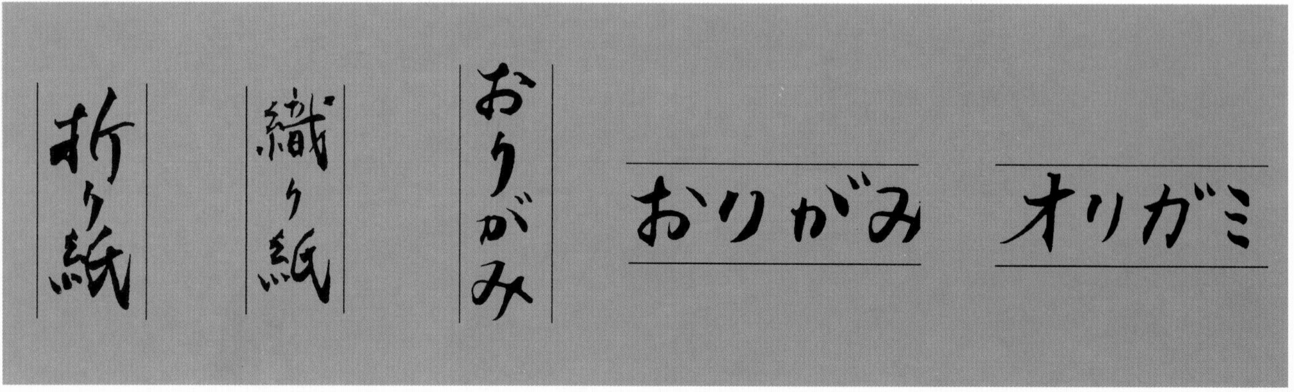

Greek Soccer Ball

This traditional ball form originated in ancient Greece. At that time, the ball was woven from soybean vines and was therefore very solid. It was used in playing a type of handball that was a tough men's sport, because of the danger of injury.

For the plaited model shown here, the materials and techniques are altered. You will learn on page 20 why this form is described as a Soccer Ball.

Folding Instructions

① Length: 29 cm (11.5 inches); cut 6 strips

Width: 1.5 cm (5/8 inch)

1 cm

1 cm

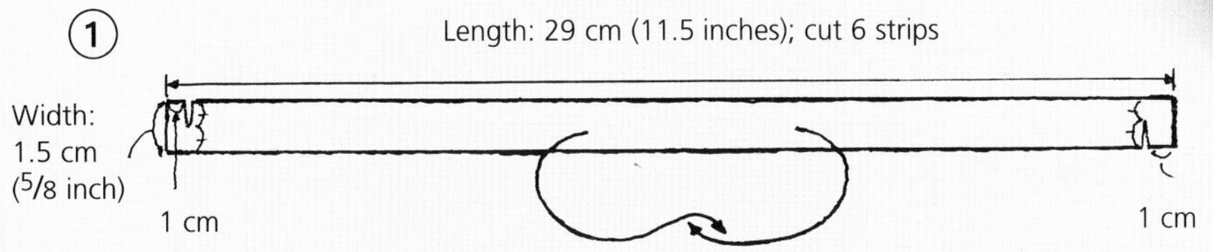

② 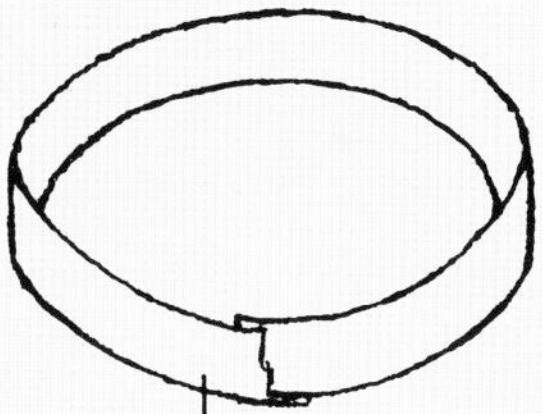 Make 1 strip into a ring by interlocking the ends.

③

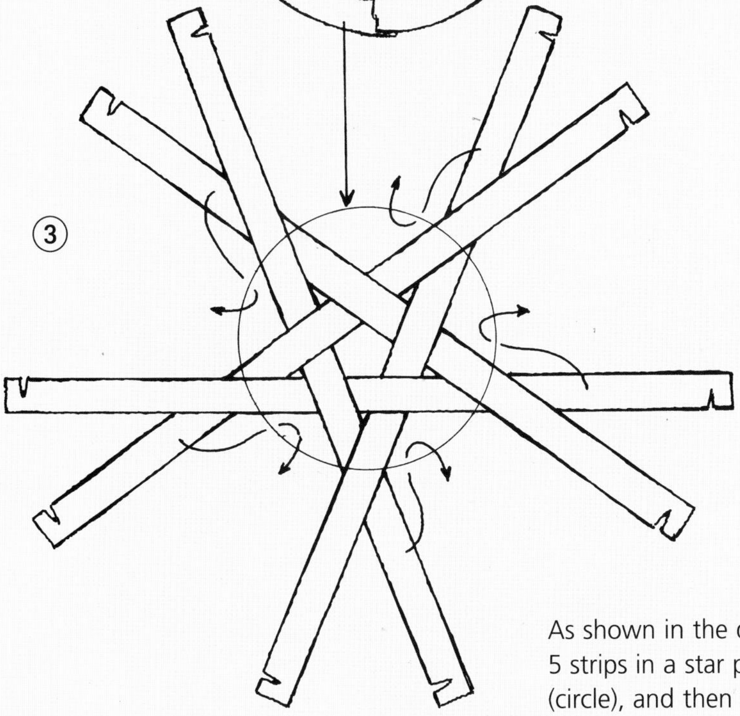

As shown in the drawing, lay out the remaining 5 strips in a star pattern, place the ring on top (circle), and then weave all the strips into a ball.

The Soccer Ball: A Dodecahedron

In a book about traditional international sports, the familiar soccer ball shape from page 19 is described as a "dodeka ball." The Greek word *dodeka* means twelve, a number that refers to the ball's basic geometric shape, the dodecahedron. A dodecahedron is a solid whose surface is composed of twelve regular pentagons that are all the same size. In a similar fashion, the woven model on page 19 has twelve pentagonal openings. If you look at the ball, you can also see hexagons, formed by the intersections of the strips. The hexagons are similar to the twenty white fields of a soccer ball, while the pentagonal openings correspond to the black fields. Yet the model is not a dodecahedron, it is rather, like a soccer ball, a truncated icosahedron.

Below you will see my solution for a true dodecahedron made from plaited paper strips.

Dodecahedron

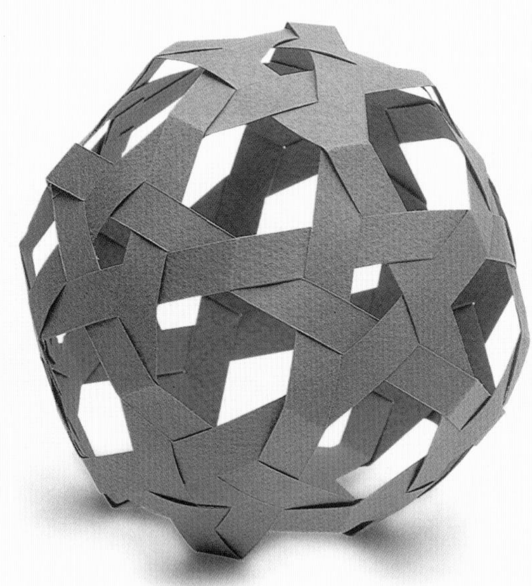

To make the dodecahedron structure more noticeable, the edges on this model are creased.

Length: 36 cm (14 3/16 inches)

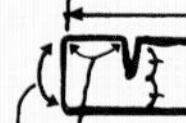

Strip width and cut distance: 1 cm (3/8 inch) each

10 strips

Strip width and cut distance: 1 cm (3/8 inch) each

For this model you will need 10 long, thin strips of paper. Closely examine the photos. For this, instructions deliberately are not given. If you were successful in making the Soccer Ball on page 19, you probably will be able to make the Dodecahedron.

The Regular Polyhedrons

Now that you are already acquainted with the Dodecahedron (page 20), one of the five basic geometric shapes, you are prepared to build the remaining four regular polyhedrons from paper strips: the Tetrahedron, Hexahedron (Cube), Octahedron, and Icosahedron. The weaving technique is based on the development of the *Configuration Puzzle* invented by Toshiaki Betsumiya.

I give you only the basic materials and photos of the finished models in order to leave you the joy of finding the solutions by yourself.

Tetrahedron

6 strips
length: 15 cm (6 inches)
width: 1 cm (3/8 inch)
Slits are 1 cm from the ends of the strip.

Hexahedron (Cube)

6 strips
length: 16 cm (6 5/16 inches)
width: 1 cm (3/8 inch)
Slits are 1 cm from the ends of the strip.

Octahedron

6 strips
length: 23 cm (9 inches)
width: 1 cm (3/8 inch)
Slits are 1 cm from the ends of the strip.

Icosahedron

12 strips
length: 40 cm (15 3/4 inches)
width: 1 cm (3/8 inch)
Slits are 1 cm from the ends of the strip.

Froebel Star

The Japanese Pandanus Star shown earlier has its counterpart in the European tradition: a star plaited out of paper strips, developed by the previously mentioned founder of kindergartens, Friedrich Wilhelm August Froebel. Many people already may know this star; however, you will find the instructions here so that you may become more familiar with the new origami techniques of binding, plaiting, and weaving.

In contrast to the Pandanus Star, the Froebel Star must be folded; it also has 16 points, four more points than the Pandanus Star.

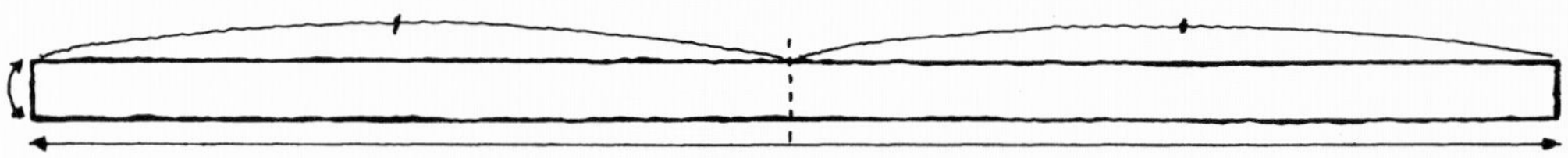

4 strips

Width: 1.5 cm (9/16 inch)

Length: about 40 cm (15fi inches)

Bend the four strips in half and, as shown in illustration 1, assemble the folded strips into a cross.

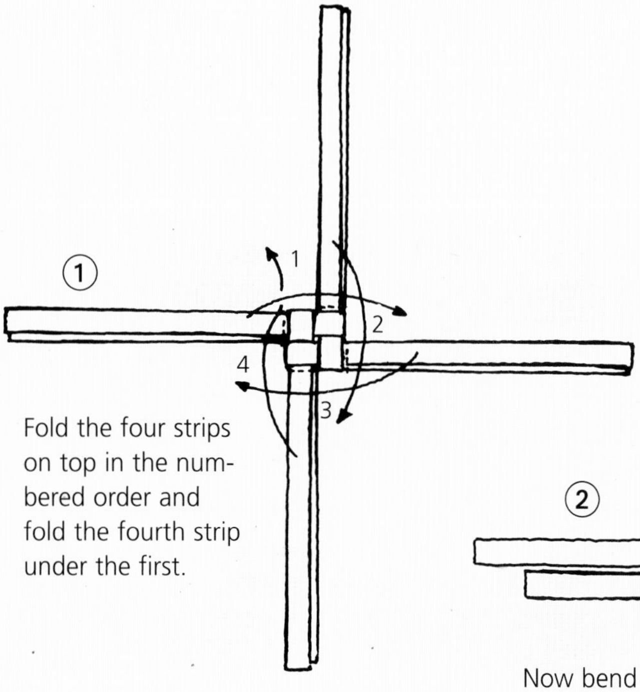

①

1 2 3 4

Fold the four strips on top in the numbered order and fold the fourth strip under the first.

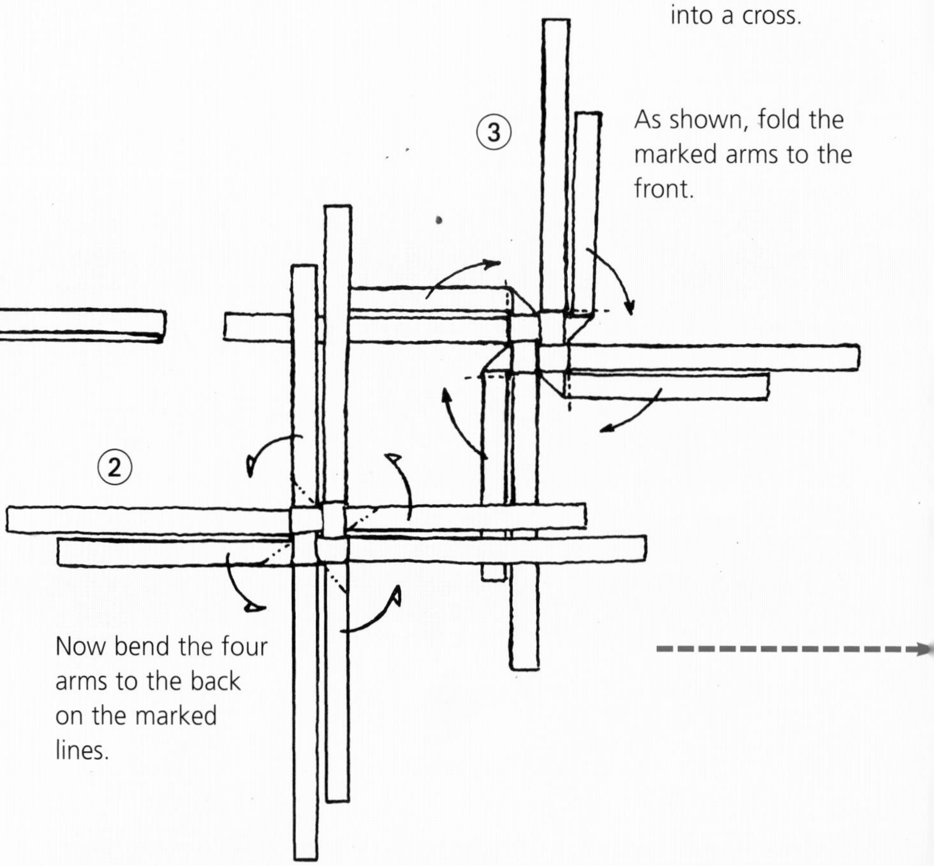

②

Now bend the four arms to the back on the marked lines.

③

As shown, fold the marked arms to the front.

For 7: To form a three-dimensional point, open a valley fold created in Step 5 halfway, pull the end of the strip under the loop of the middle cross-section and through the folded triangular point made in Step 4. The side of the strip visible in the drawing must lie on top at the start of this. The illustrated fold lines should show the direction in which to bend the strips, but they should not be folded. Repeat this with the three other strips.

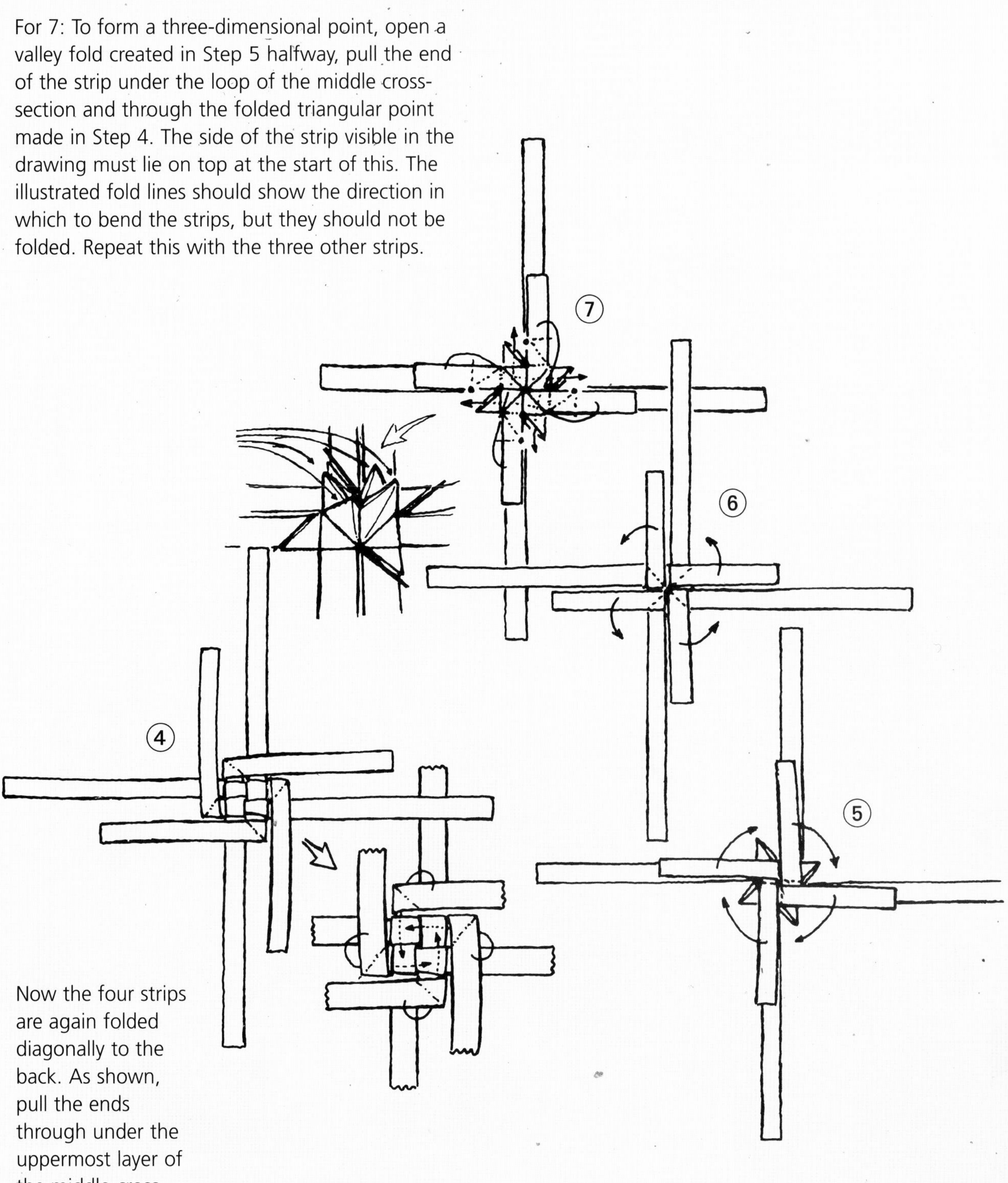

Now the four strips are again folded diagonally to the back. As shown, pull the ends through under the uppermost layer of the middle cross.

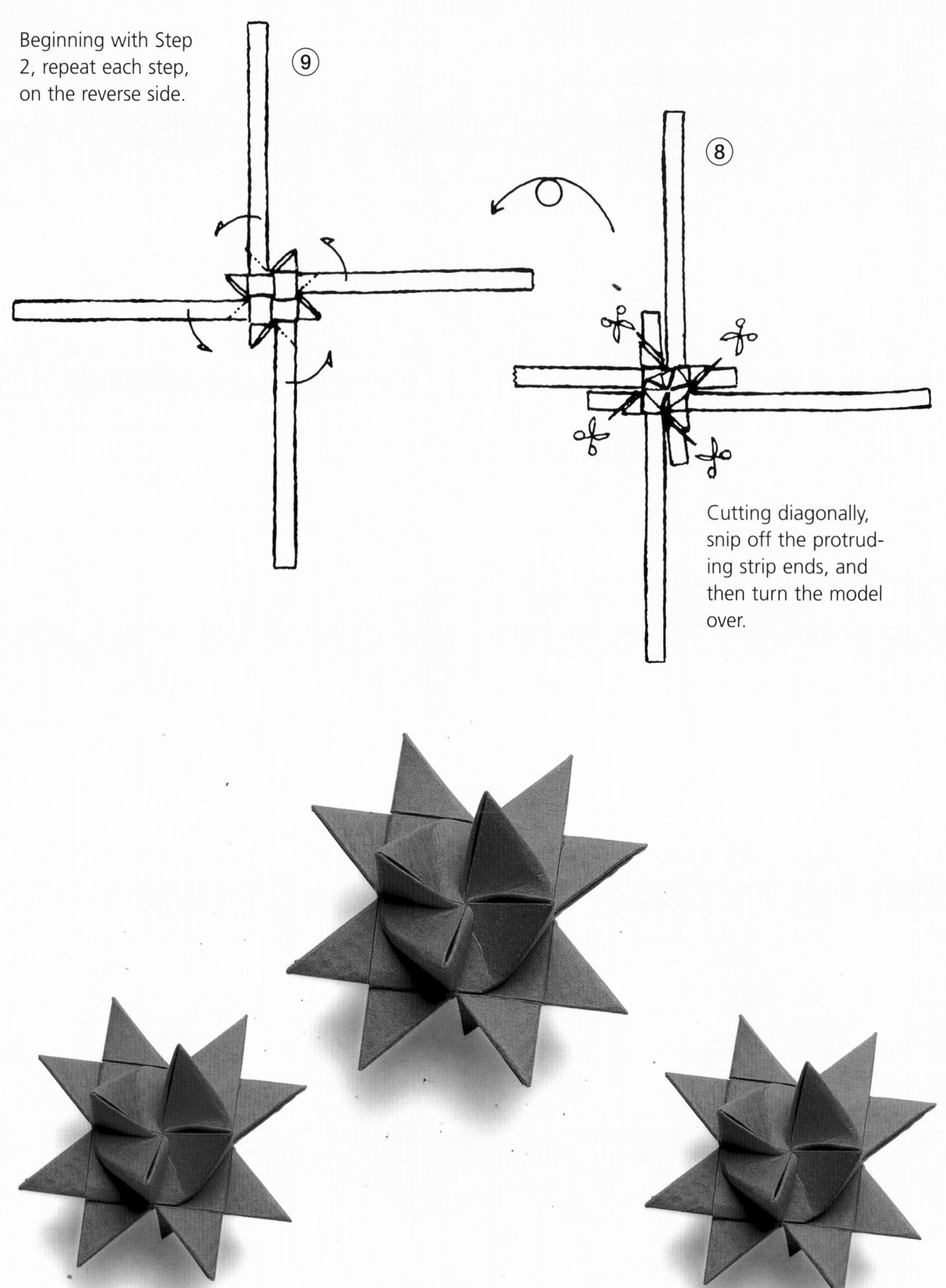
Beginning with Step 2, repeat each step, on the reverse side.
9
8
Cutting diagonally, snip off the protruding strip ends, and then turn the model over.

Knot Techniques

Along with the binding, plaiting, and weaving of paper strips, there remains still another shaping technique: the knot technique. Heinz Strobl discovered and developed this origami technique, in which geometric function and aesthetics are combined. He jokingly called this method "knotology," or the science of the knot.

The basis of this technique is to tie a paper strip into knots; from this a regular pentagon develops. Theoretically, if one ties knot after knot on an endless band of paper, a pattern develops and other geometric shapes may be created. These could be viewed as a single strip of paper that is neither cut nor glued, and therefore it does not violate the traditional rules of origami.

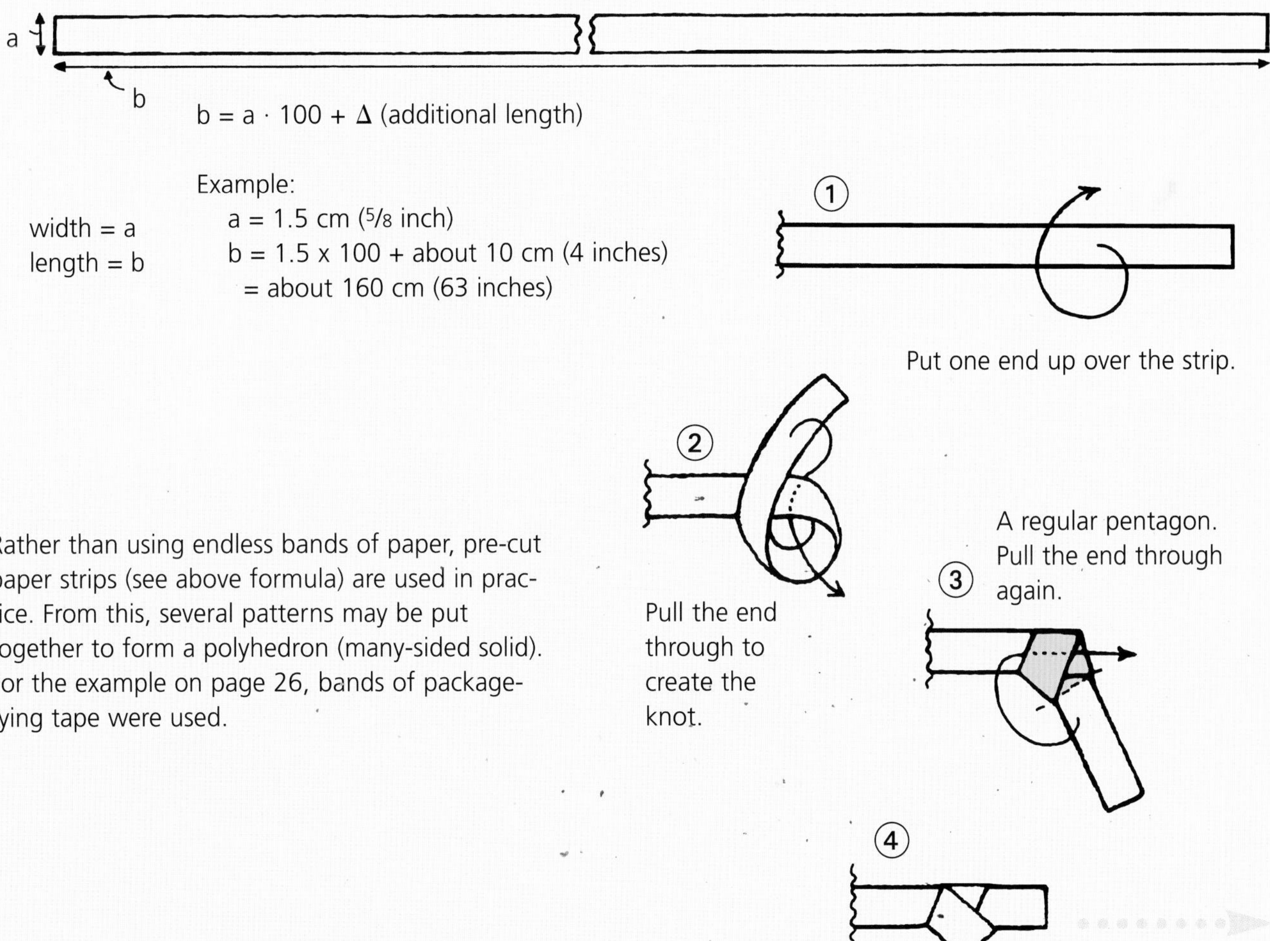

$b = a \cdot 100 + \Delta$ (additional length)

width = a
length = b

Example:
a = 1.5 cm (5/8 inch)
b = 1.5 x 100 + about 10 cm (4 inches)
= about 160 cm (63 inches)

Put one end up over the strip.

Pull the end through to create the knot.

A regular pentagon. Pull the end through again.

Basic knot pattern.

Rather than using endless bands of paper, pre-cut paper strips (see above formula) are used in practice. From this, several patterns may be put together to form a polyhedron (many-sided solid). For the example on page 26, bands of package-tying tape were used.

Sphere 94
by Heinz Strobl

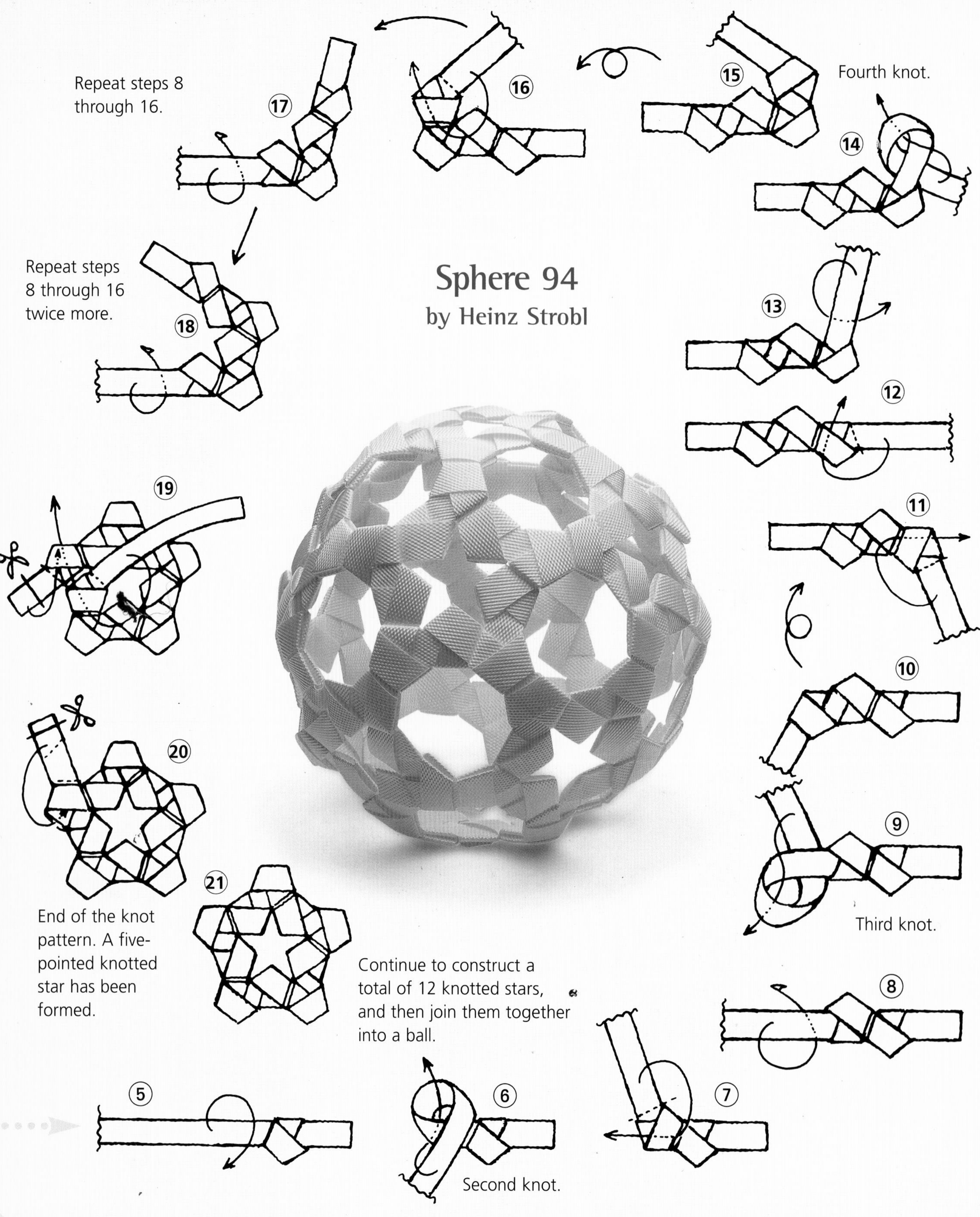

Repeat steps 8 through 16.
17
16
15
Fourth knot.
14
Repeat steps 8 through 16 twice more.
18
13
12
19
11
10
20
9
Third knot.
21
End of the knot pattern. A five-pointed knotted star has been formed.
Continue to construct a total of 12 knotted stars, and then join them together into a ball.
8
5
6
7
Second knot.

Chapter 2 Imagiro and Origami: The New World

What is an imagiro? Imagiros are people who live scattered throughout the world, extraordinary individuals who are brave combatants in the peaceful origami revolution. More about imagiros is explained in the following pages. The origin and meaning of the term can be found on page 36.

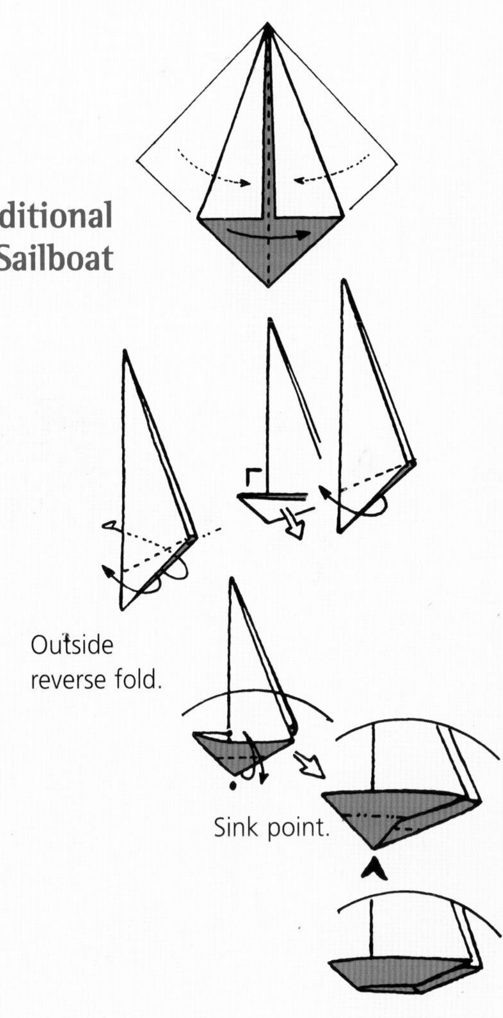
Traditional Sailboat
Outside reverse fold.
Sink point.

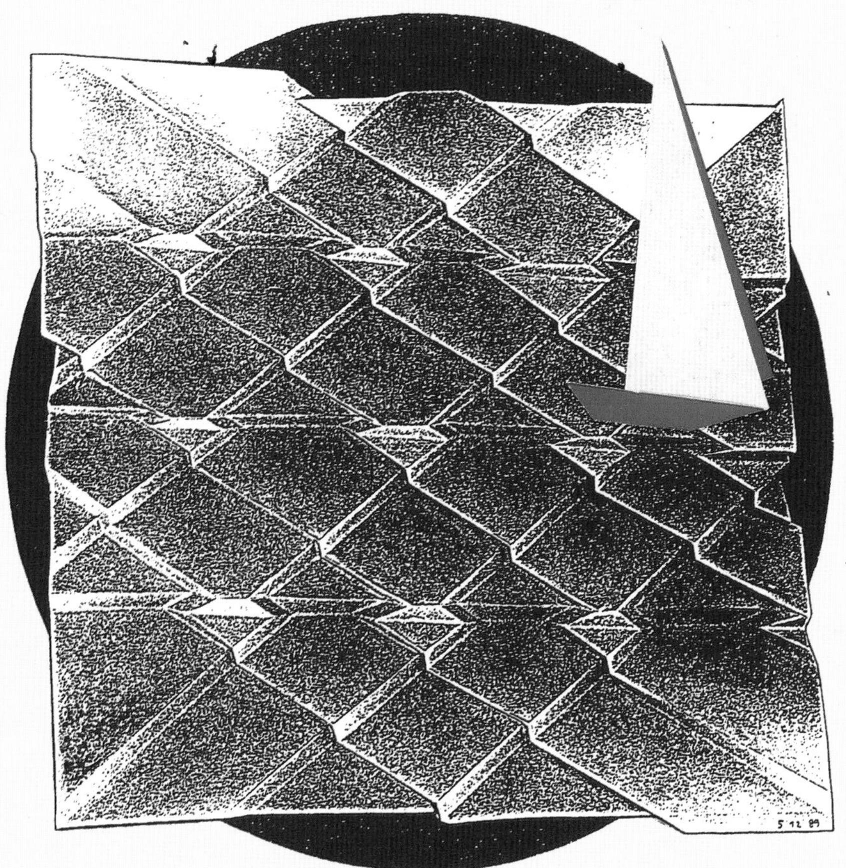

Untitled
by Paulo Taborda Barreto

Broken and Incomplete Folds

Origami implies designing with straight lines, or so it has been thought until now, but using rounded forms and curved surfaces revitalizes the technique, as we showed in the first chapter.

There remains one more unbelievably simple technique, which consists of making a fold on only one edge of the paper. At the center of the paper where the fold ends, the area will begin to curve, creating a bow in the paper.

Less is sometimes more. This is what the English origami artist Paul Jackson taught me. The form that he conceived as an example of this technique (see photo) consists of a single fold, which ends in the paper's center. This gave me the idea of starting with, for example, only a half fold. The flying dove is also based on this principle. If the fold touches only one edge of the paper, a flowing, dynamic curve on the surface and paper edge are formed.

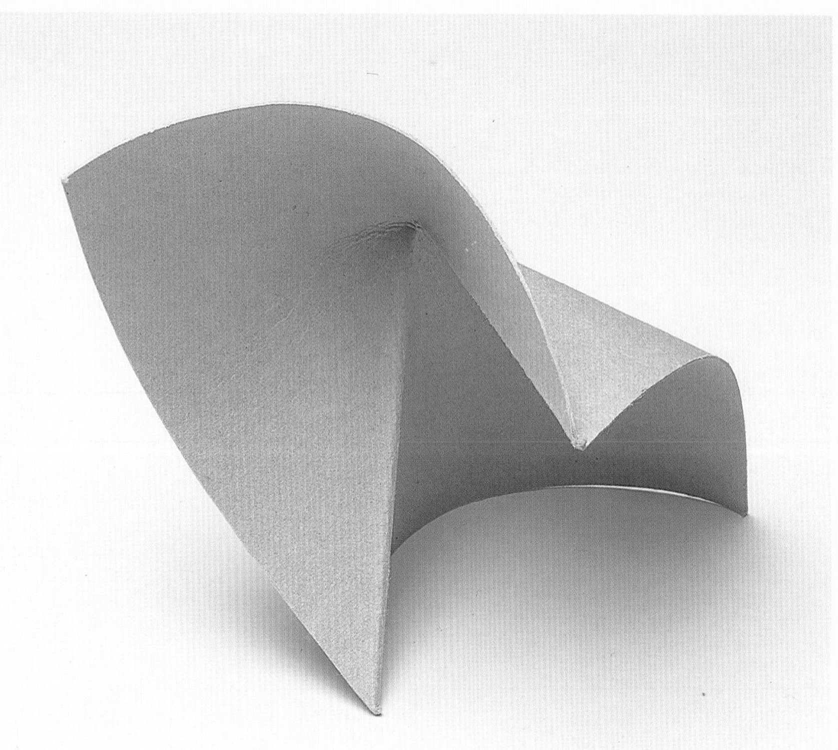

Curve Construction (by Paul Jackson)
The form consists of a single fold, which is bent in one place. The model is made of moistened cardboard, a material rarely used in origami projects.

Flying Dove

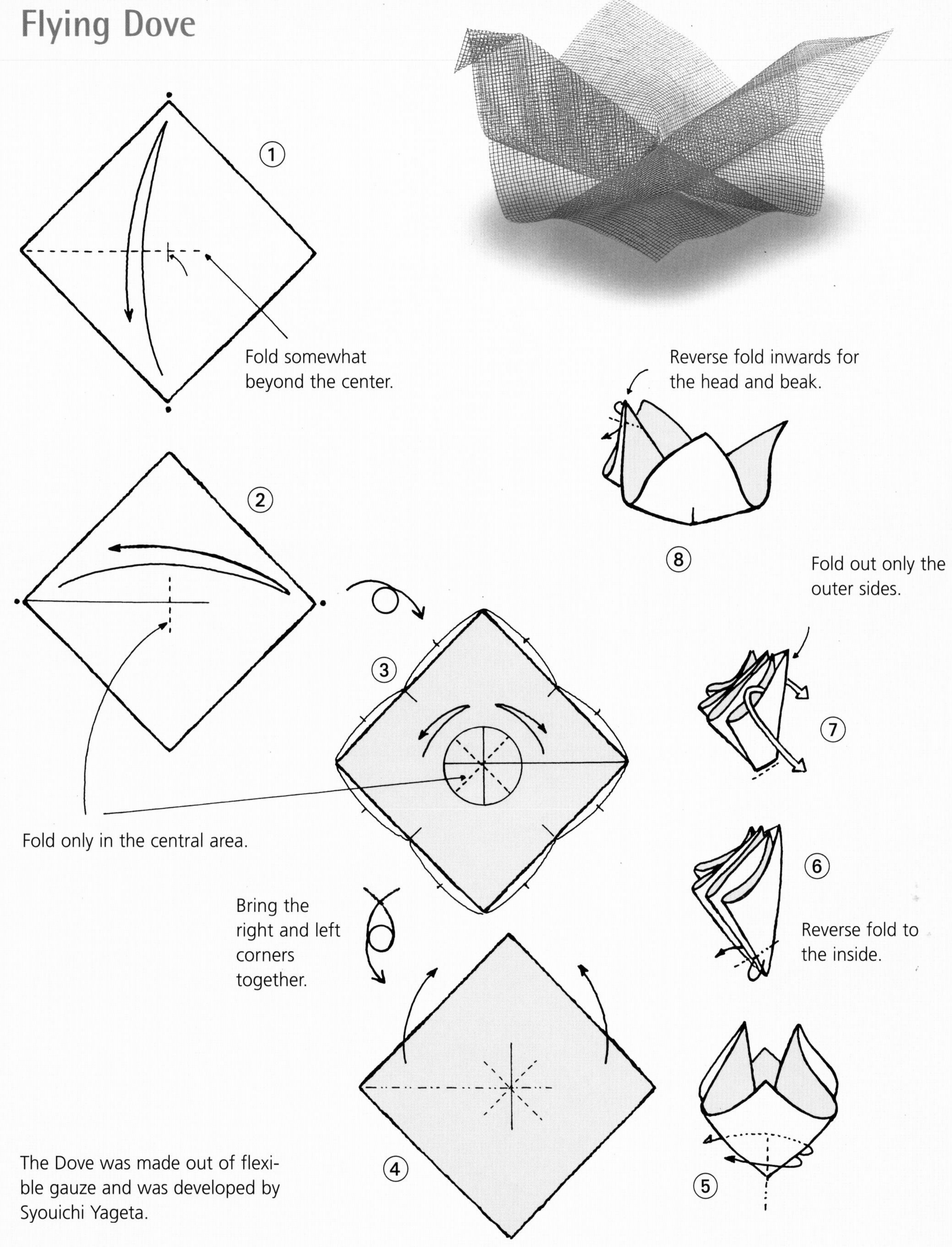

1
Fold somewhat beyond the center.
2
Fold only in the central area.
3
Bring the right and left corners together.
4
5
6
Reverse fold to the inside.
7
Fold out only the outer sides.
8
Reverse fold inwards for the head and beak.

The Dove was made out of flexible gauze and was developed by Syouichi Yageta.

Cutting

Cutting is considered a crude violation of the conservative rules of traditional origami. Traditionally, when comparing similar origami creations, a model without any cuts is much better regarded than one with cuts.

That might sound sensible, but on further reflection it can't be considered correct, because the aesthetic quality of a work cannot be judged by the technique used to make it. That would be the same as claiming that a ceramic vessel produced by hand building is better than one turned on a potter's wheel.

Here, two interesting aspects of origami are combined — on one hand, a clever solution to technical problems and on the other, creative aesthetic design.

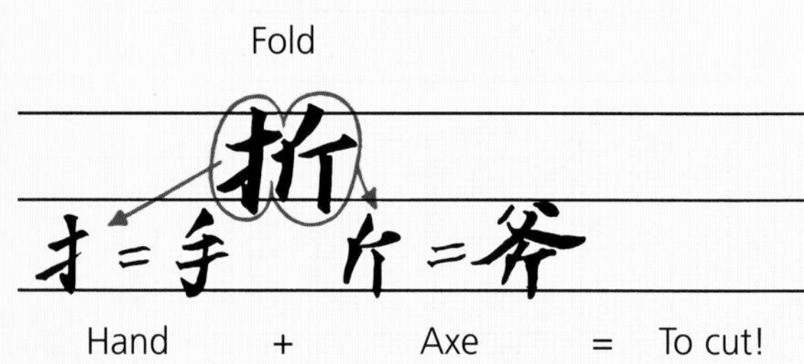

Folding = Cutting?

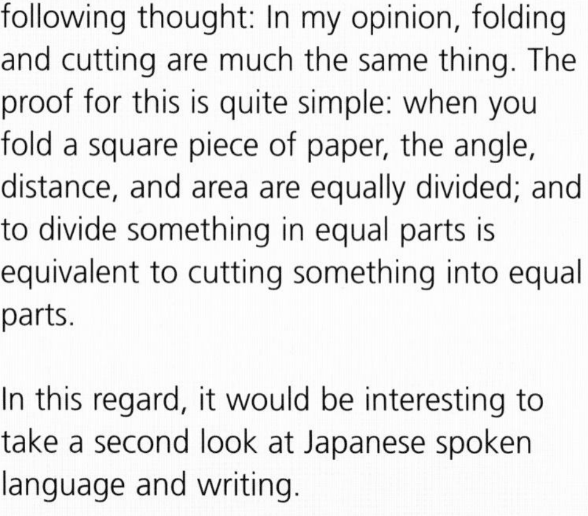

So that we can get this technical hurdle out of the way, I'd like you to consider the following thought: In my opinion, folding and cutting are much the same thing. The proof for this is quite simple: when you fold a square piece of paper, the angle, distance, and area are equally divided; and to divide something in equal parts is equivalent to cutting something into equal parts.

In this regard, it would be interesting to take a second look at Japanese spoken language and writing.

In Japanese writing, the characters for "to fold" are 扌 and 斤. In the second example, the leftmost character 扌 = 手 = hand; the right character 斤 = 斧 = axe, which originally meant "to cut."

There is also a phonetic equivalence: the verb *oru* = ("to fold") 折 is also pronounced *setsu,* which means "to cut" *Setsu* we can see also means "to cut" (切).

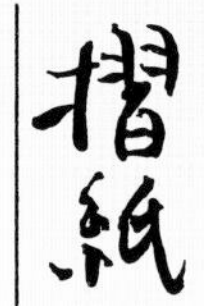

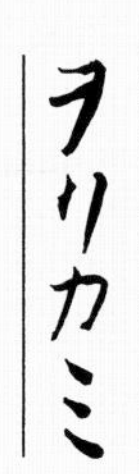

おりがみ

ヲリガミ

オリガミ

紙おりもの

折紙細工

Masterpiece with Cuts

Imoseyama. This beautiful, traditional design has been known since 1797, the year the book *Senbazuru-Orikata (A Thousand Origami Cranes)* was published. The Crane shown is made with different colors on the front and back sides of the paper.

Siamese Twin Crane

Instructions on page 41 for the single crane (Orizuru).

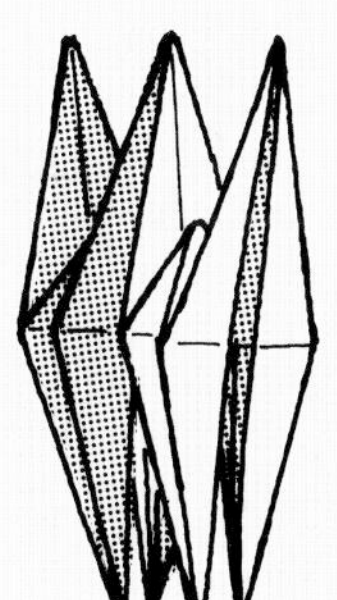

These will become the heads (little arrows).

Whale

Instructions on page 38

These creations have a long tradition, and their creators were surely imagiros....

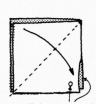

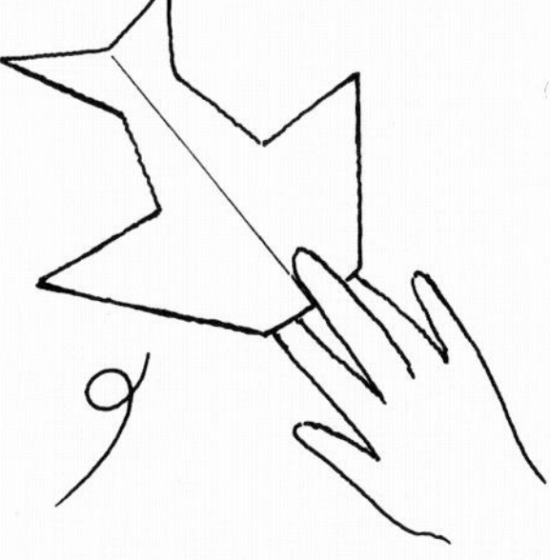

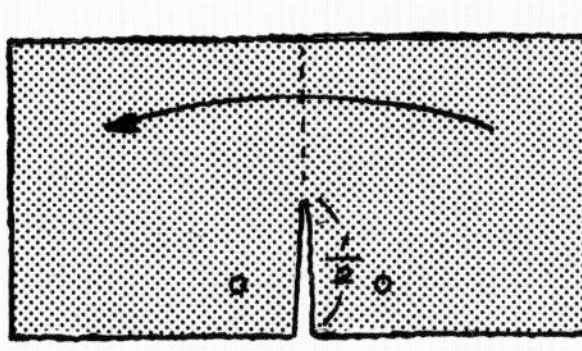

For Siamese Twin Crane, start with rectangle of side ratio 1: 2. Each side is folded into a Bird Base. Finish both Bird Bases into Cranes (steps 9–12 on page 41) and you will get the Siamese Crane (photo above).

Paper Plane, Swallow Type

Instructions on page 41

Cutting as a Stage of Development

In order to free origami from the persistent refusal to use cutting, I give yet another argument, combined with a practical example.

In Japanese kindergartens, origami paper is used as a teaching aid. Naturally, the children begin with cutting or tearing paper, since this method is easier than folding and also teaches the correct method of handling scissors.

Since we see that cutting is easier than folding, it seems quite natural that when first designing with paper, the simpler technique should be employed. Those who are already familiar with folding will soon realize that in some respects cutting can be more difficult. The results of a cut are harder to estimate and impossible to change if done incorrectly.

Nevertheless, this technique serves as a useful means when needed and when it makes sense.

The development of the different Dragonfly models shown on these pages should illustrate this principle.

I folded the first Dragonfly (Model A) from a single sheet of paper, but it came out very thick, which bothered me. I then employed the cutting technique, and a new form emerged (Model B). This Dragonfly is wonderfully slim, and the body and wings have different colors. Model C is a variation of Model B and is my favorite Dragonfly.

Model A Dragonfly

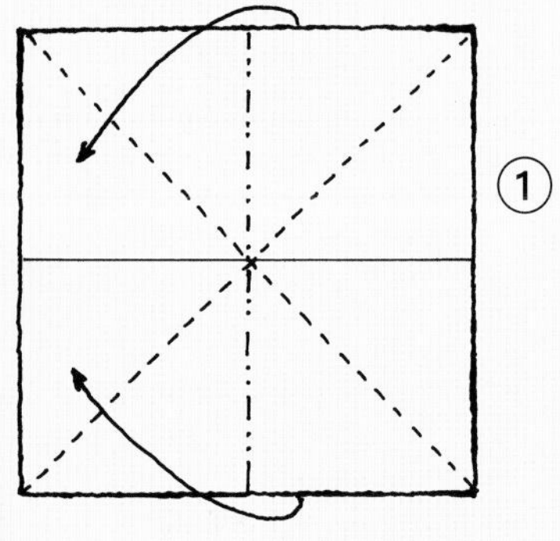

It is only possible to fold Model A from very thin paper.

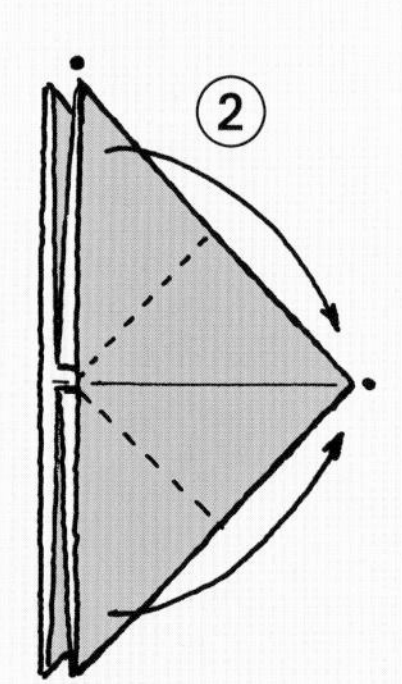

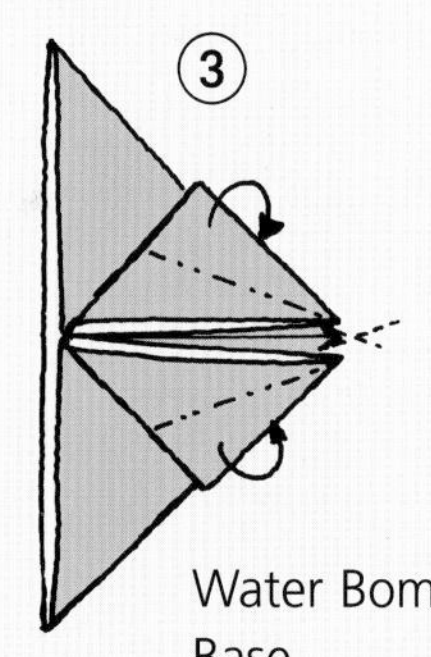

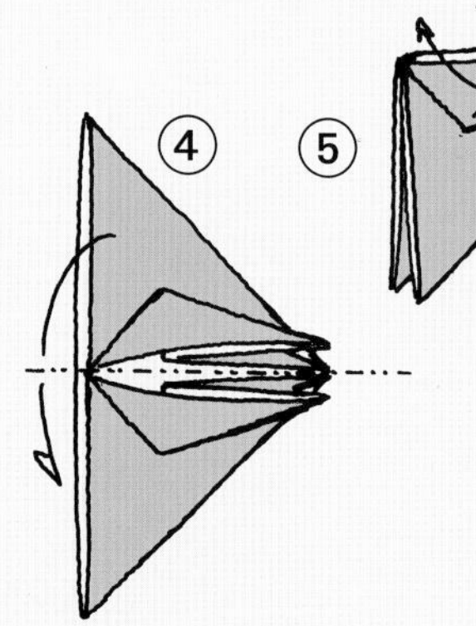

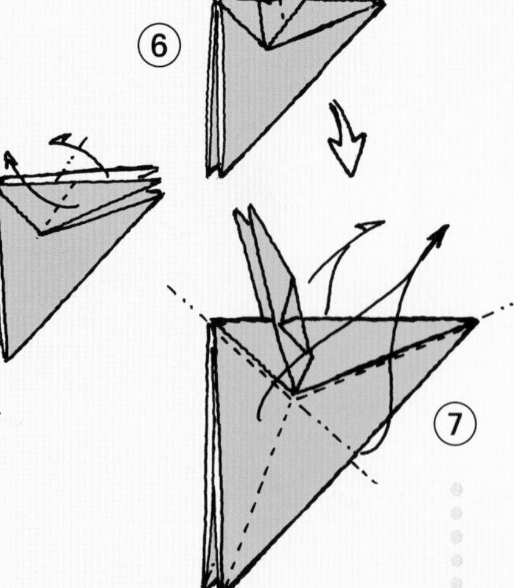

Three Dragonflies and Their Evolution

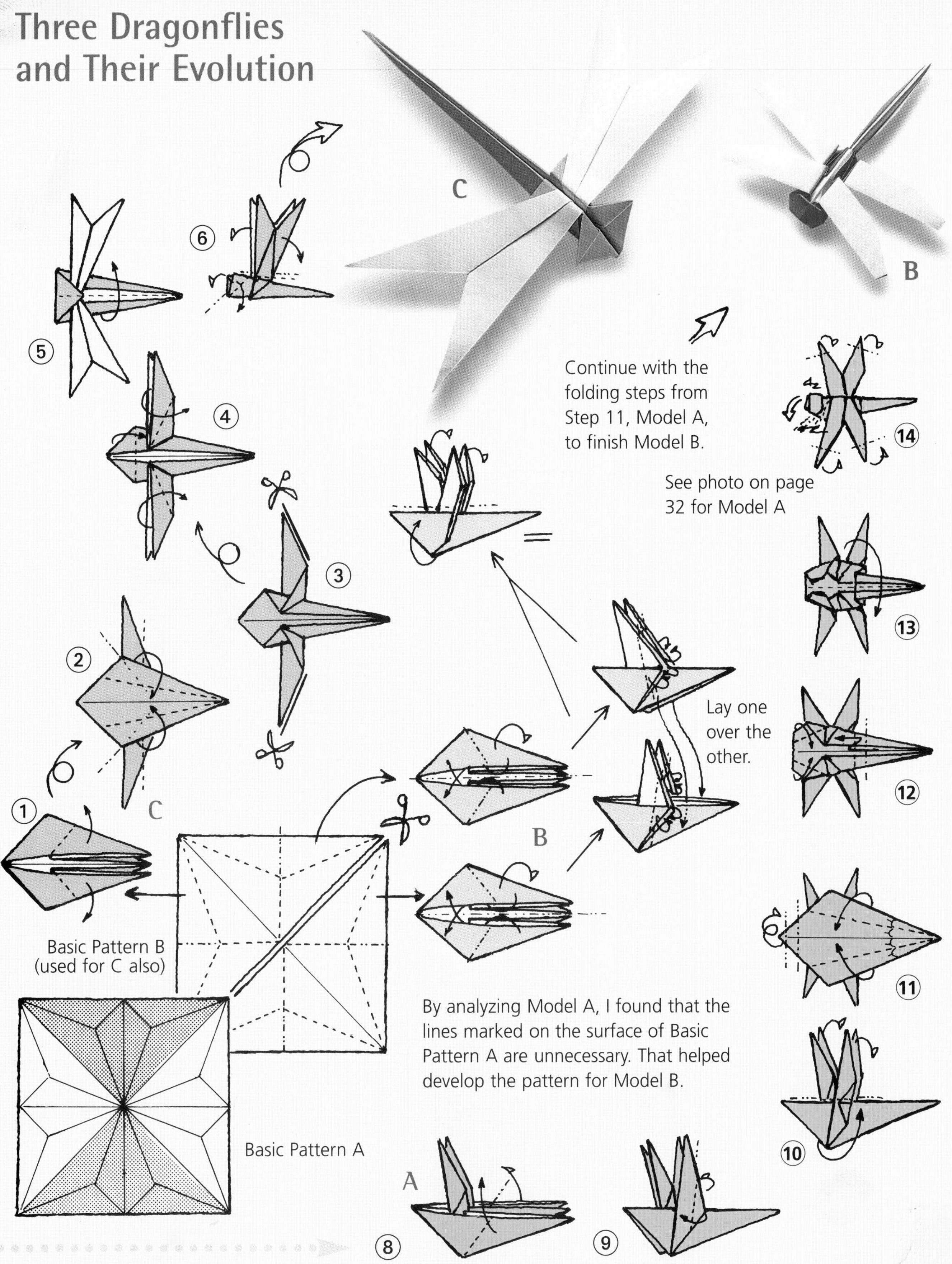

C
B
5
6
4
3
2
1
C
B
A
8
9
10
11
12
13
14
Continue with the folding steps from Step 11, Model A, to finish Model B.
See photo on page 32 for Model A
Lay one over the other.
Basic Pattern B (used for C also)
Basic Pattern A
By analyzing Model A, I found that the lines marked on the surface of Basic Pattern A are unnecessary. That helped develop the pattern for Model B.

Breaking Symmetry

The basic shape used in origami is the square, which allows for the easiest construction, unlike the rectangle, where length and width must be determined, or the triangle, where angle and side length are needed. Because the square is symmetrical, it may be folded left, right, over, under, symmetrically and also front to back; however, if you intentionally fold a square asymmetrically, a new, totally unexpected outcome can be achieved.

You can see an example of this method in the photo below. Vector, created with only two fold lines of slightly broken symmetry, has a dynamic, flowing expression. The Mouse on page 35 also illustrates this principle: front and back are basically symmetrical, yet the symmetry has been intentionally broken (Step 6).

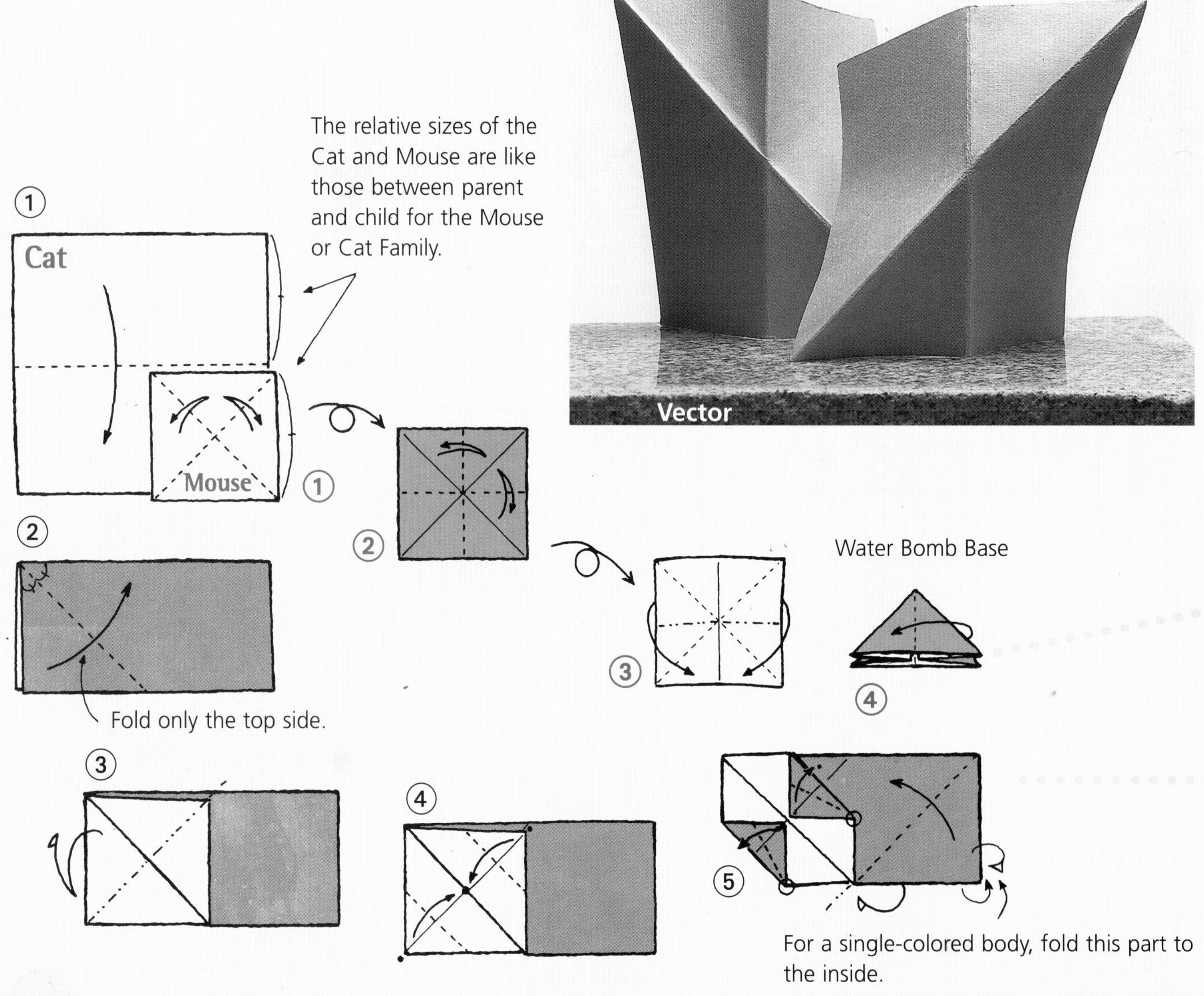

The relative sizes of the Cat and Mouse are like those between parent and child for the Mouse or Cat Family.
1
Cat
Mouse
1
2
2
Fold only the top side.
3
Water Bomb Base
4
3
4
5
For a single-colored body, fold this part to the inside.
Vector

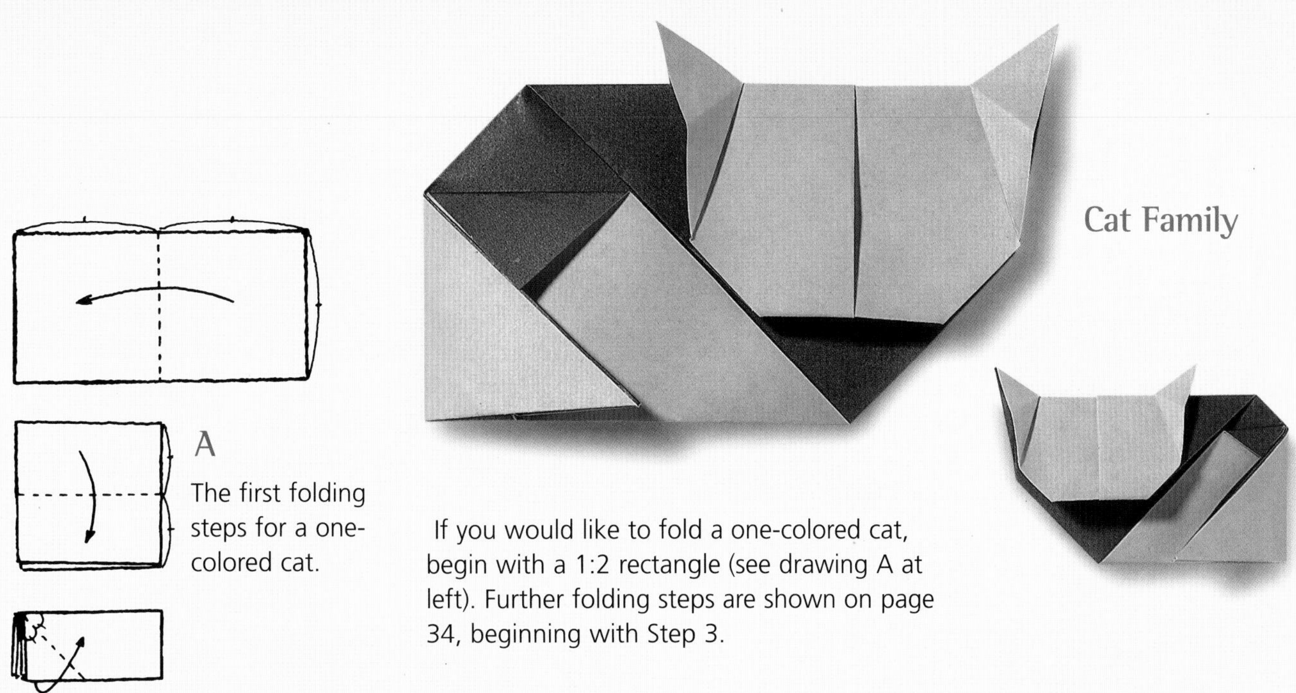

Cat Family

A

The first folding steps for a one-colored cat.

If you would like to fold a one-colored cat, begin with a 1:2 rectangle (see drawing A at left). Further folding steps are shown on page 34, beginning with Step 3.

Mouse Family

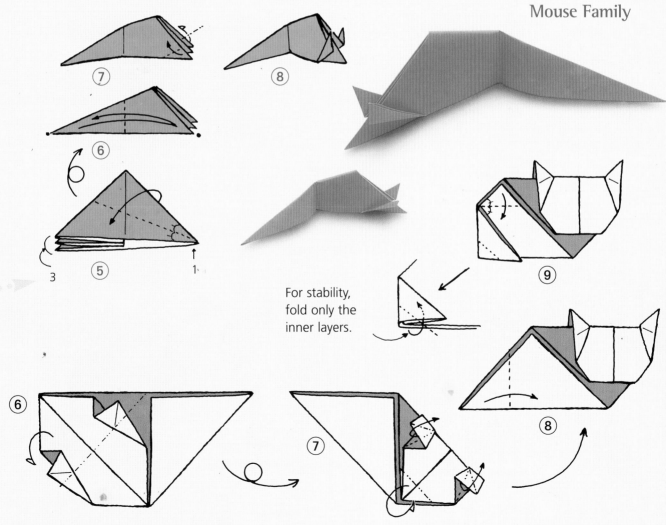

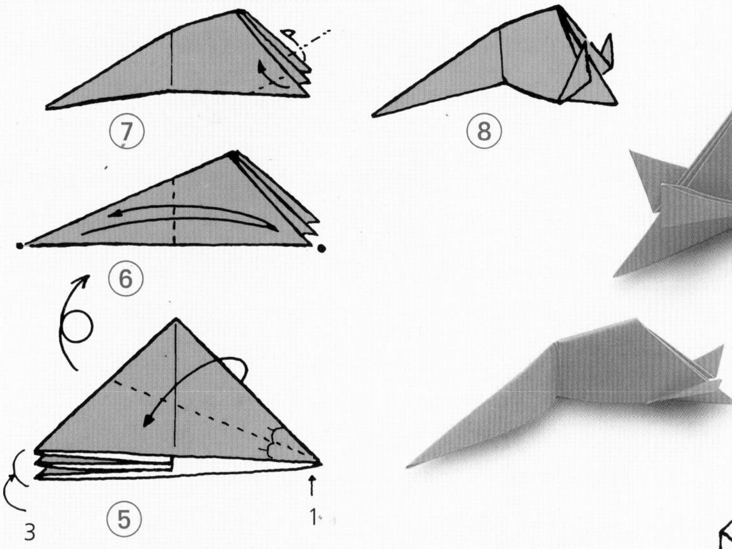

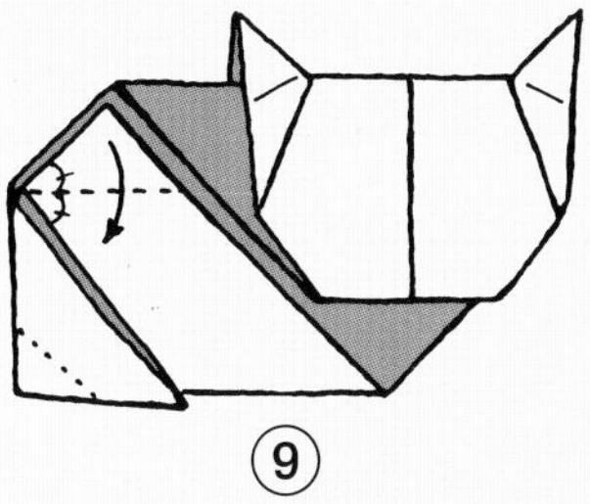

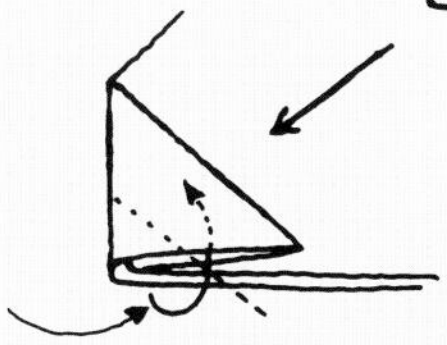

7 8

6

5 3 1

9

For stability, fold only the inner layers.

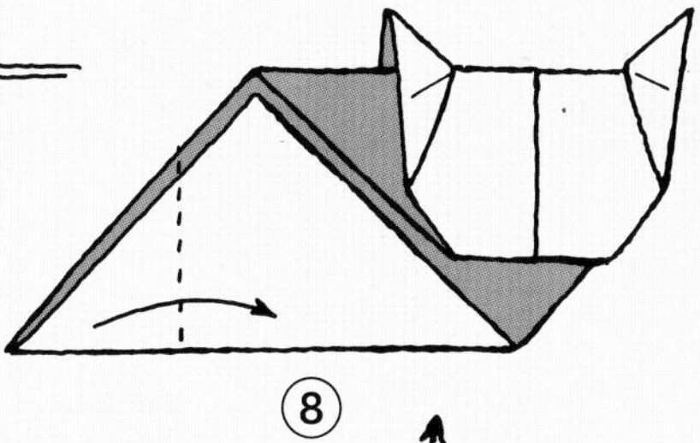

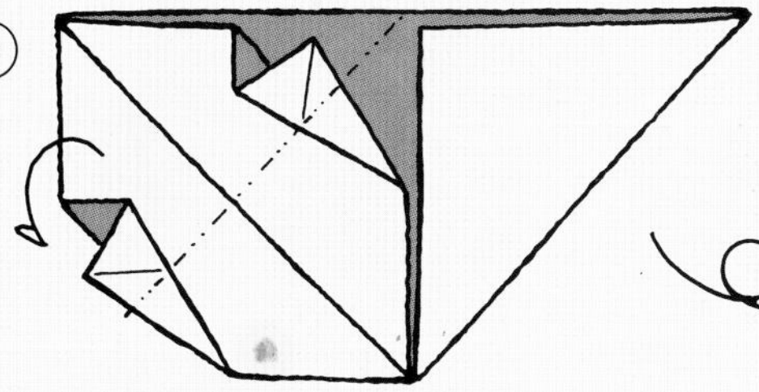

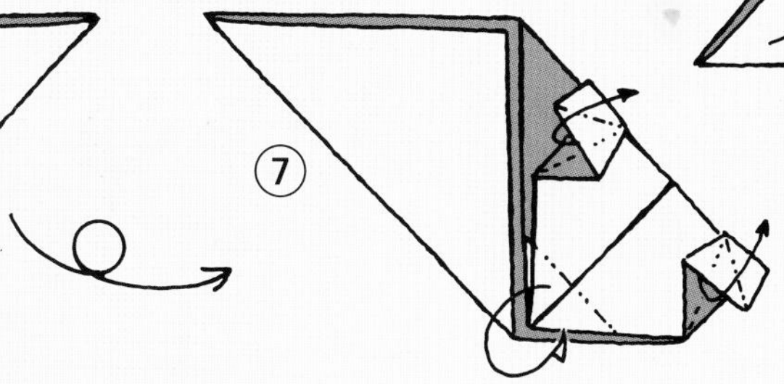

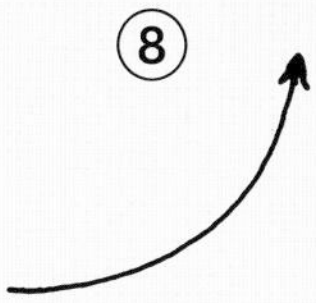

6 7 8

Experimenting with Shape

At my first meeting with Thoki Yenn in March 1993, he suddenly asked me, "Do you know imagiro?" To my ears it sounded like *Ima-jiro,* and so I thought he was inquiring about a Japanese first name. Jiro is, in Japan, a common name for the second born son of a family. The firstborn is frequently called Taro or Ichiro. The third son is named Saburo; the fourth, Shiro, and the fifth, Goro. But *Ima* (Japanese for "now") *jiro*? I could not think of anyone with such an unusual name.

At that, Thoki laughed and wrote IMAGIRO on a piece of paper. When read backwards, the word ORIGAMI is revealed. A play on words, but for me it meant much more.

An imagiro is a person with imagination and an *amigo* (Spanish for "friend"). Many of my wonderful origami friends are imagiros. The notion of image is also included. This play on words showed me a deeper meaning of origami (image = picture, shape in English and French) and also inspired me to develop a new creative method called shape association. You will find some examples on the following pages.

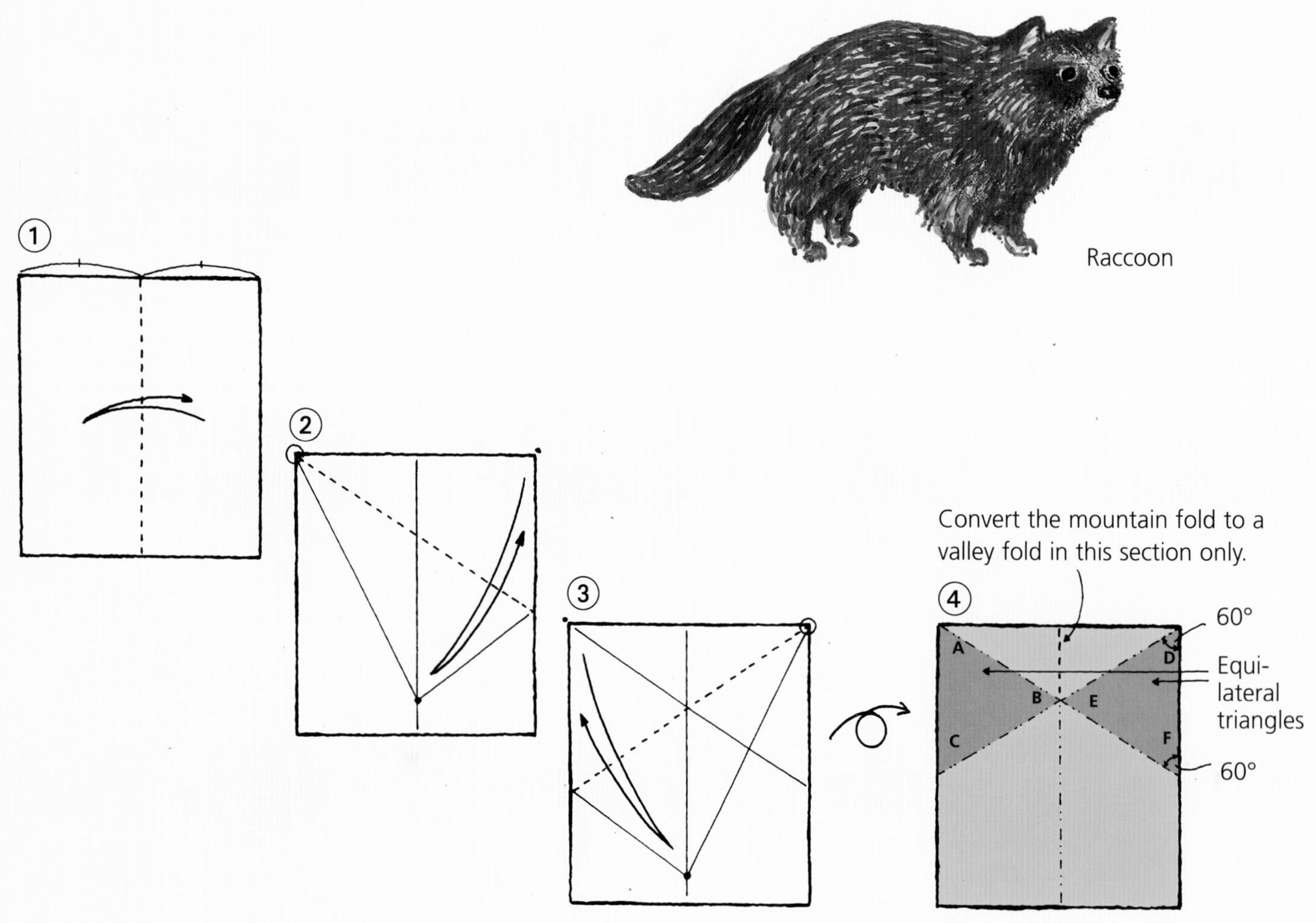

Which Shape Do You See?

The photo on this page shows a figure with only three fold lines. What do you see in this form? I have recognized many different animals — for example, a cat, an owl, and also the legendary Tanuki, who is a constant companion in Japanese fairy tales.

If you look closer at steps 2 and 3 on page 36, you will see the division into thirds, under accurate conditions, of the angle on the middle fold; therefore triangles ABC and DEF are equilateral triangles.

Ordinarily this folding is only viewed as an aspect of geometry. Now, as I had honored its aesthetic qualities, I could also imagine new possibilities for designs.

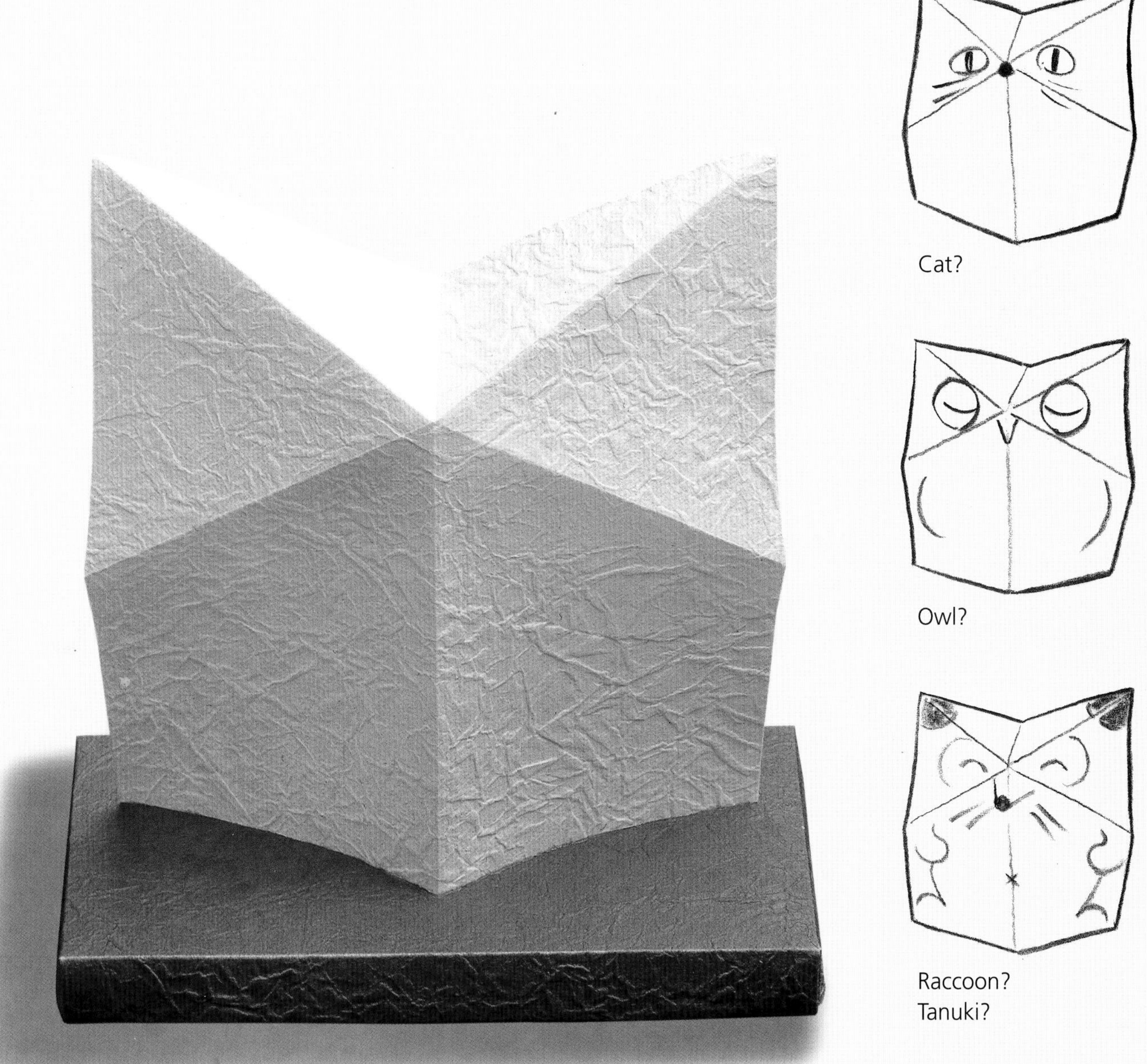

Cat?

Owl?

Raccoon?
Tanuki?

Shape Association

In the beginning, I feared that only I could perceive these shapes, but I occasionally showed these creations to other people, and almost everyone could see something definite as well.

My new, very simple creative method, shape association, works as follows:

To begin with, only fold a couple of lines; then examine the result in a half open position. Now let your imagination run free. You will definitely be able to find a few images. Now add some supplementary folds to strengthen the image and transform your fantasy shape into a perfect new creation.

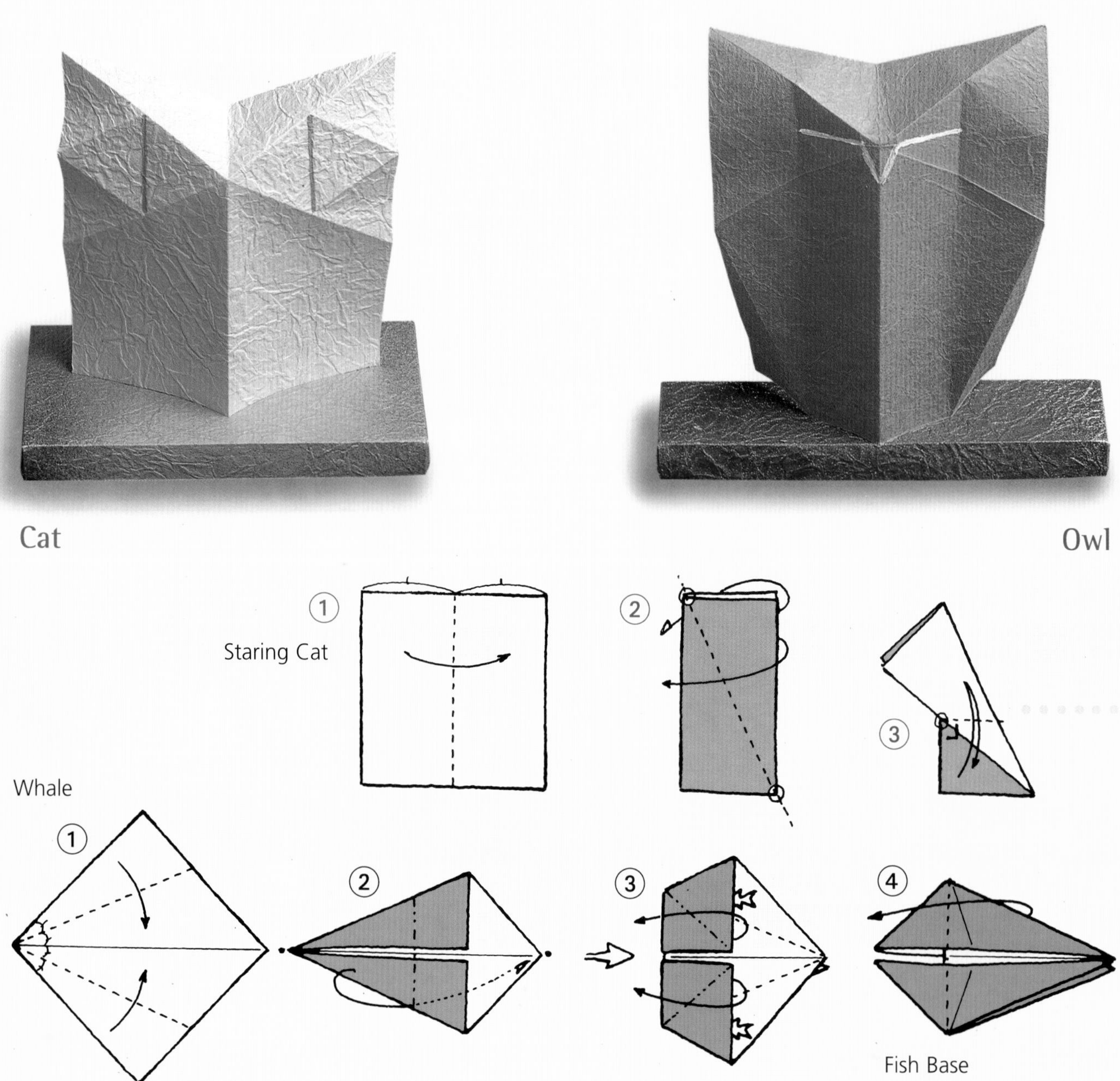

Cat

Owl

Painting and Gluing

Unfortunately, the supplementary lines that help strengthen the image often disturb the original shape. As an alternative, I propose a technique that, until now, has been criticized and therefore excluded: moderate painting of lines (see page 38).

In the search for more transformational possibilities for my Cat design, I have found still more expressive folds. A particular concern was to emphasize the distinctive expression of the eyes by emphasizing the folds. For this I have used a technique even more despised in origami than cutting; gluing colored paper onto the base.

Yes, yes, I can already hear loud opposition from the many friends of origami ... but in this manner it was possible to create a satisfactory image. And, to repeat: it is through such small steps over the boundaries of classic origami that an unbelievable expansion of design and aesthetic horizons is possible.

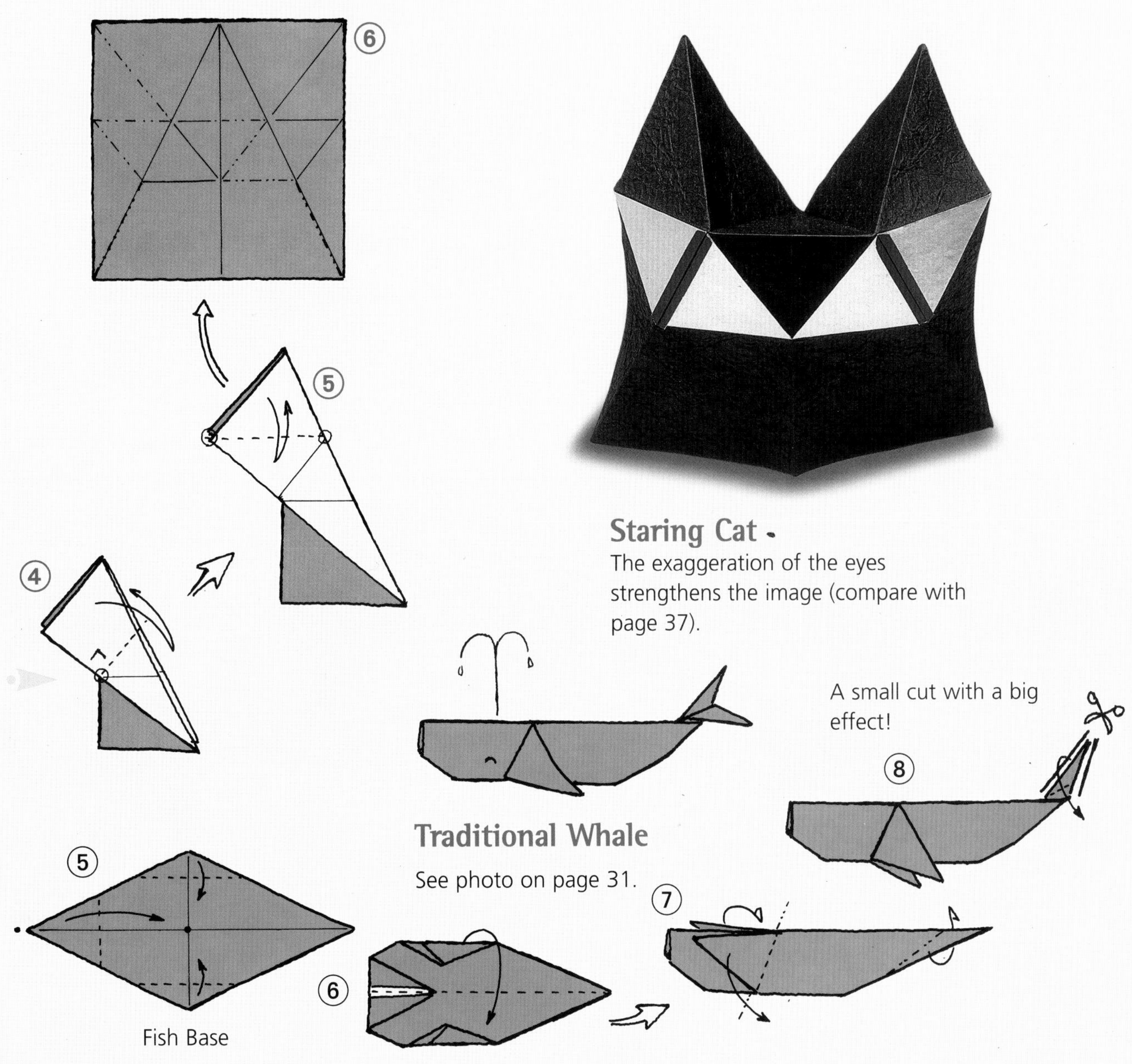

Staring Cat - The exaggeration of the eyes strengthens the image (compare with page 37).

Traditional Whale

See photo on page 31.

Playing with Basic Forms

On this page you will find more examples of the technique of shape association. This method is so simple! Just let your imagination play and visualize your own particular image. Very original creations can come from this. *Your* works — designs that have never been seen before!

For Bird Base

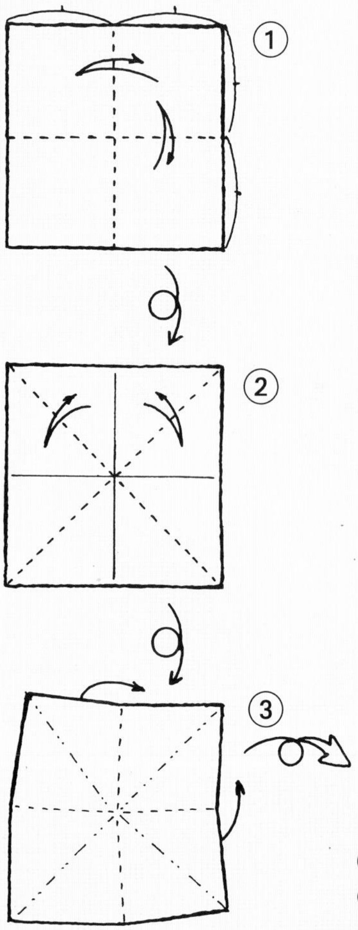

1

2

3

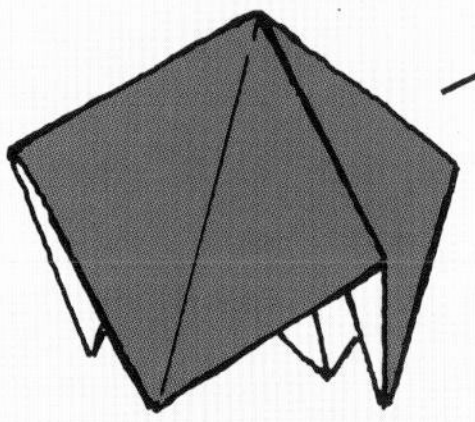

Overturned Bird Base:
Common mammal shape.

Specific Shape:
Bear

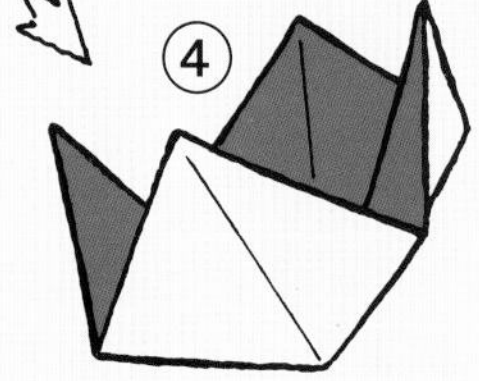

4

Bird Base Form:
Common bird shape.

My Orizuru model is less abstract and seems somewhat more realistic than the masterly Orizuru in traditional style on page 41.

Specific Shape:
My Orizuru

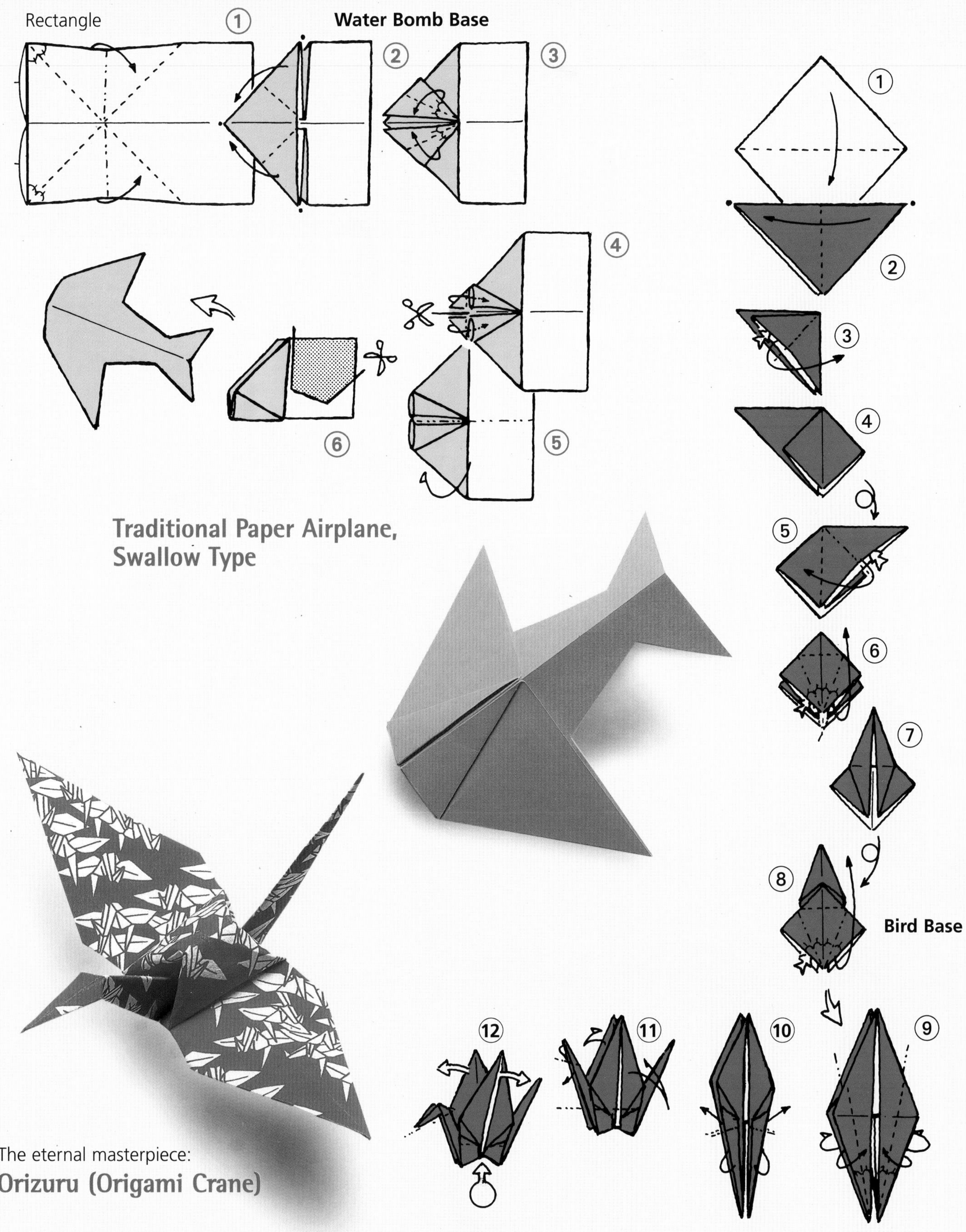

Traditional Paper Airplane, Swallow Type

The eternal masterpiece:
Orizuru (Origami Crane)

Using Transparency

Please examine the three masterpieces in the photo below. Model A is a Cat's Face, Model B a Tato (small box), and Model C is a Snowflake. But why should they be masterpieces; what makes them so exceptional? If you look at them from above as usual, the distinctive feature remains concealed.

The charm and brilliance of these models may be seen only if one holds them in front of light and looks through them (see photos on page 43).

Suddenly, the Cat's Face (A) gazes at us with mysterious, glittering eyes. The shape of a pinwheel is revealed in the Tato (B), and the area of the finished square is exactly one-third of the original (you can measure it). The Snowflake (C) reveals a new and multidimensional beauty. In these works, new territory is opened — a wide field for additional design possibilities.

Cat's Face
by Francesco Miglionico

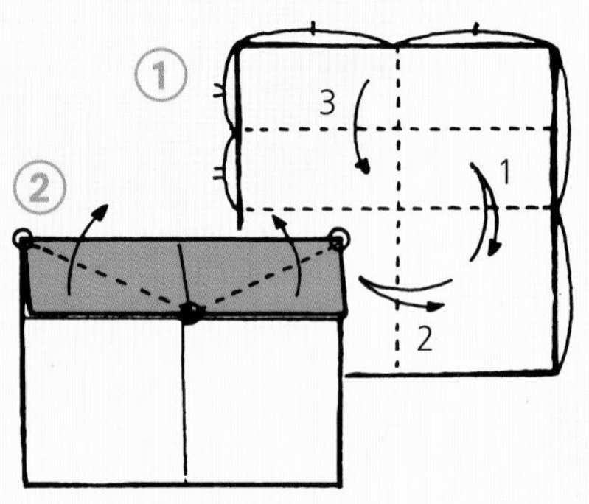

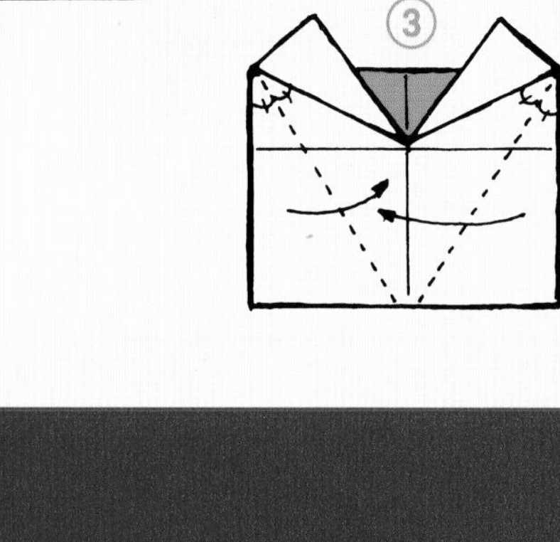

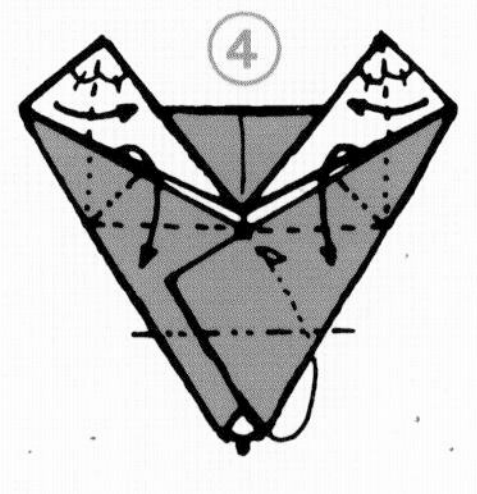

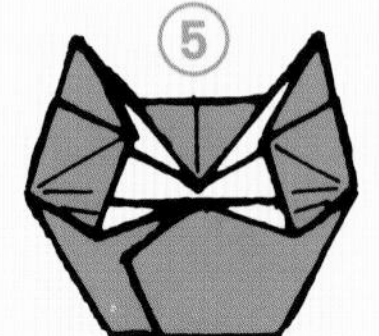

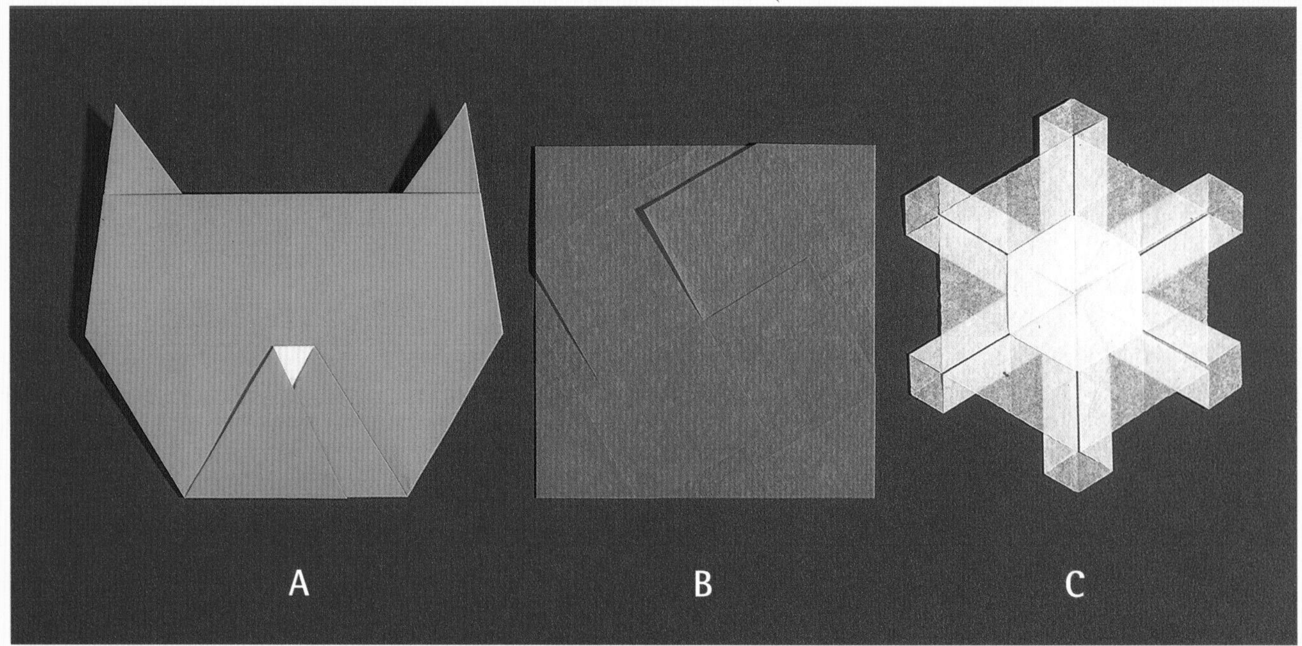

Small Box (Tato)
by Mitsue Fushimi

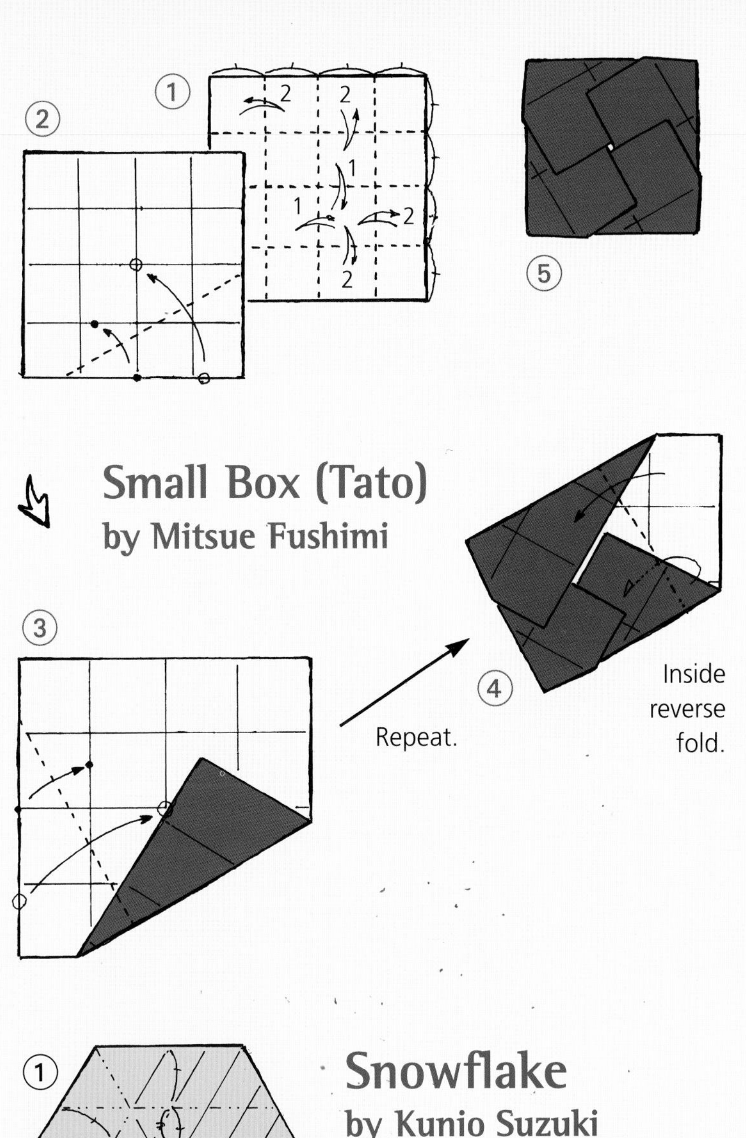

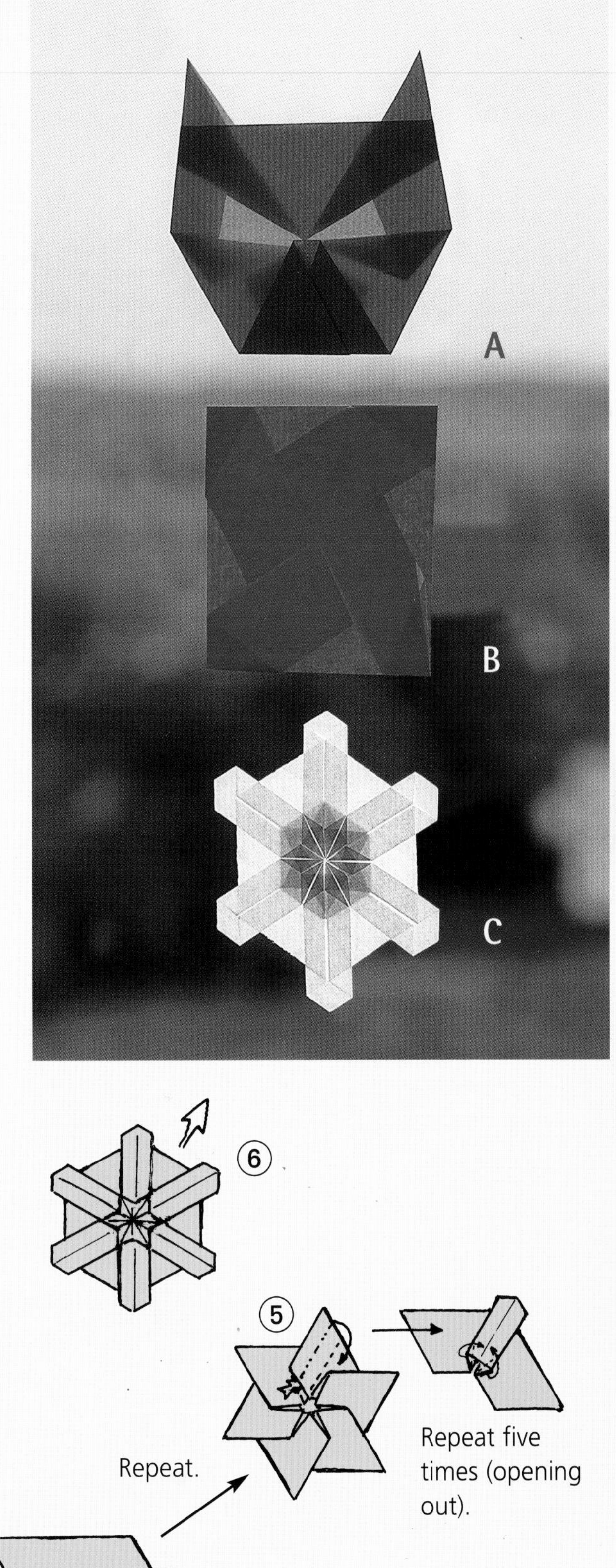

Repeat.
Inside reverse fold.

Snowflake
by Kunio Suzuki

Instructions for a regular hexagon are on page 64.

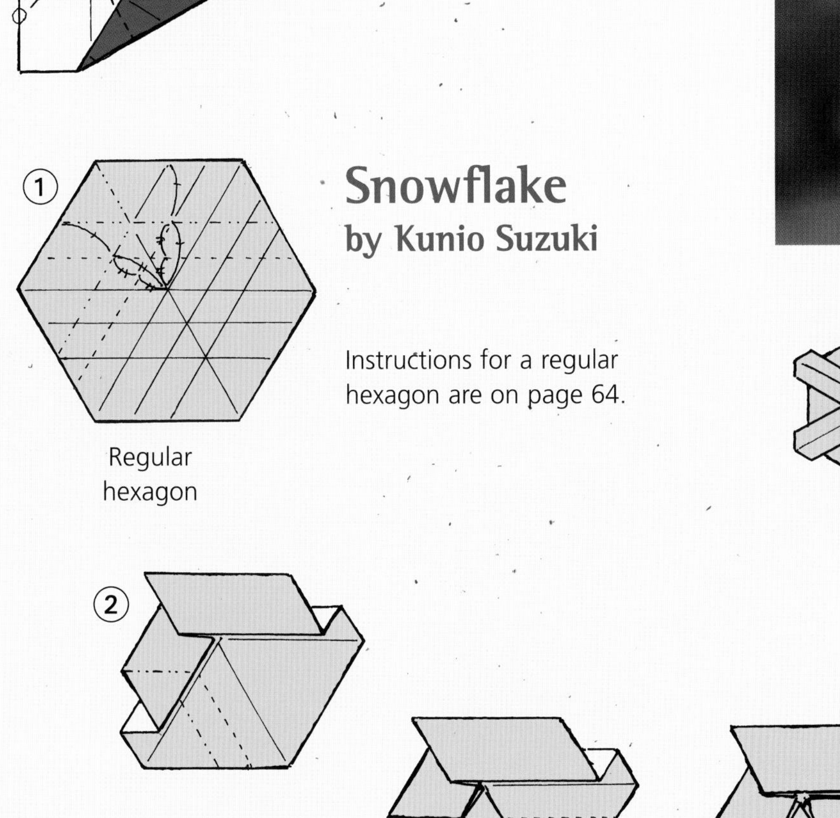

Repeat.
Repeat five times (opening out).

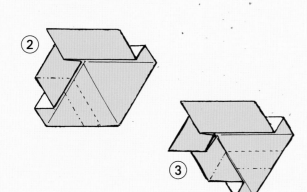

The Beauty of Hidden Patterns

Here you see a few of the Snowflake patterns designed by Professor Kunio Suzuki. For the folds, *saiten-shi,* an especially thin, handmade *washi* paper developed by Sumio Tajima was used. By these means, two aesthetic aspects are combined in the object: the beauty of form and of the material.

Suzuki's Snowflakes open even more aesthetic horizons. This will be shown with the Snowflakes in Part C.

If you look at the translucent pattern of a finished Snowflake model, you can distinguish regions with different translucency, resulting from the different numbers of overlapping layers of paper. The patterns at the top of page 45 (Part A) classify the translucency patterns of a Snowflake in a systematical way. The black parts in each individual diagram mark the regions in which a definite number of layers are overlapping. The small (subscript) numbers indicate the numbers of overlapping layers (e.g., D_{1a} indicates one layer, D_{1b} indicates another region with one layer, D_2 indicates two overlapping layers...). By combining these patterns you can create some new ones. The middle section alone (D_5 to D_{11}) can produce more than 100 possible pattern variations; if used in its entirety, the amount could be well over 2000. Now that they are no longer concealed, a new world of beauty and design possibilities has opened, which will essentially enrich origami technique.

This would not be possible if you only pay attention to the finished shape.

Suzuki discovered even more techniques to create new patterns: If the regions that contribute to a pattern of one of the diagrams (Part A) are marked on the unfolded paper, you get a new kind of pattern, which he calls a Hidden Pattern. However, that is not all: A third type of pattern emerges if one uses the sequence in which the paper layers lie on top of each other, rather than the quantity of layers, in the process of pattern creating. The resulting Pattern Chronicle with eleven Hidden Patterns can be found on page 45 (Part B).

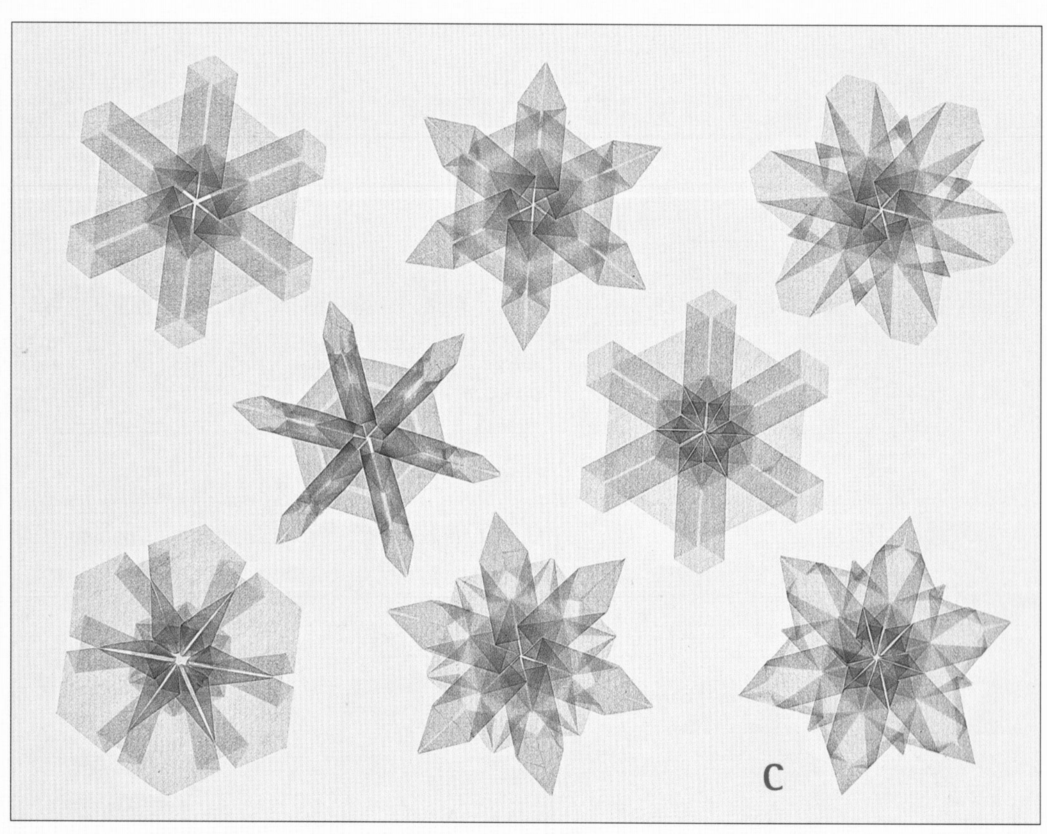

The patterns shown in Parts A and B were made by analyzing the Snowflakes in Part C.

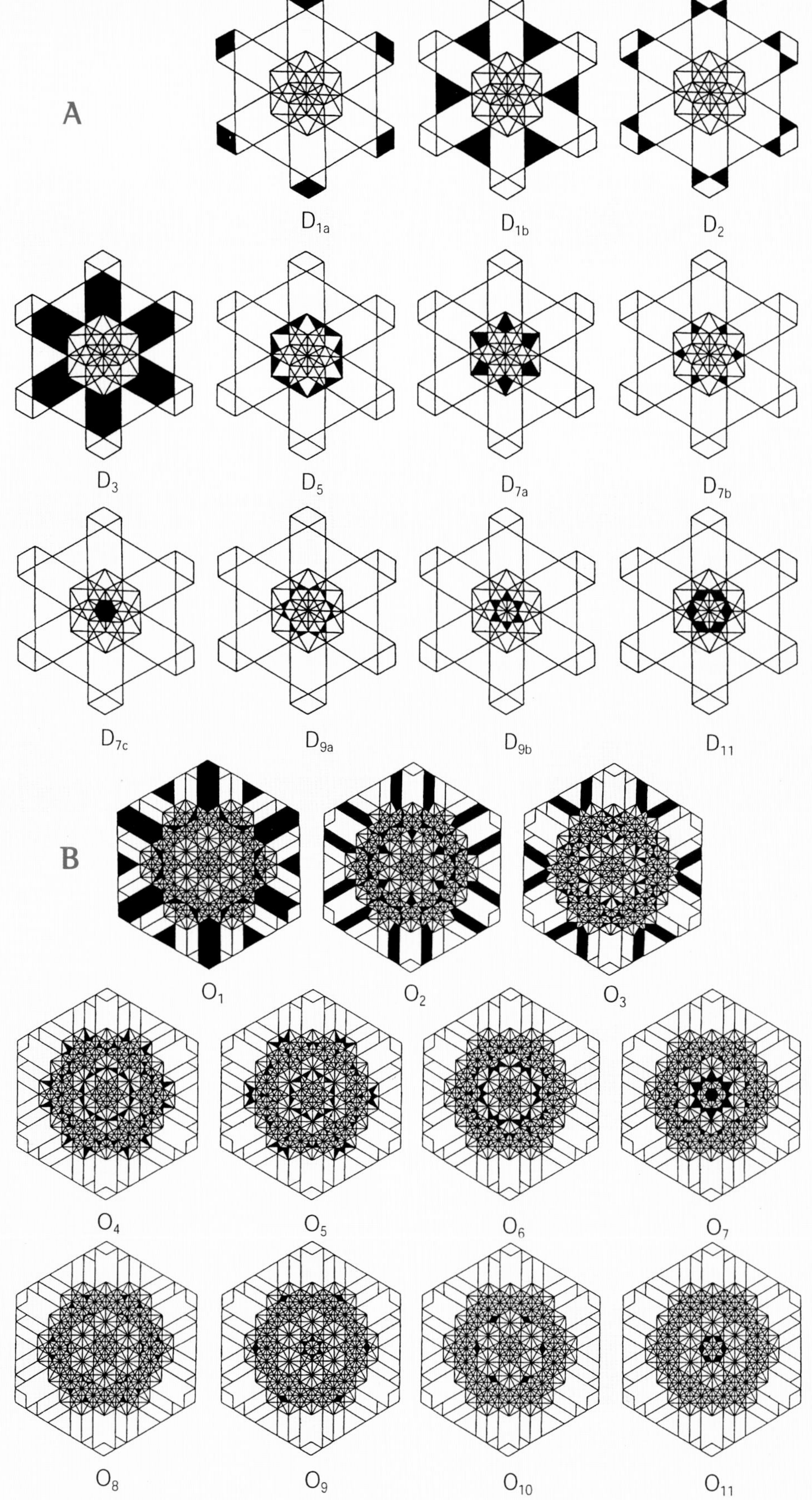

Graphics from the archive of Professor Kunio Suzuki.

The Tamatebako: A Gift Box and Its Story

As was mentioned earlier, Taro is a popular name for males in Japan, and there is a well-known fairy tale in Japanese tradition that tells a story about a man with this name and his Tamatebako.

Urashima-Taro and the Tamatebako

Once upon a time, there was a fisherman named Urashima-Taro. One day he saw children torturing a turtle which he then bought from them and released into the sea. Some time later, the turtle came back and, in gratitude, invited him to Ryugu-Jo, the magnificent palace of Oto-Hime, the Mistress of the Sea. There they honored him with a sumptuous banquet and Urashima-Taro forgot all about the time.

But after a long period, he began to miss his life on land and departed from Oto-Hime.

As a farewell gift, the Sea Queen gave him a Tamatebako as remembrance of Ryugu-Jo and said, "Never open this box. Then you will have a happy and fortunate life." (This story is similar to the one about Pandora's box.)

So Urashima-Taro mounted the back of the turtle, who brought him back to land. But when he returned, he did not recognize his village and strange people were living in his house. Urashima-Taro felt very alone and longed for Ryugu-Jo. So he opened the forbidden little box.... White smoke rose out of the Tamatebako, and Urashima-Taro was transformed into a white-haired old man. For in the box, the lost time of the past had been locked, as in the story of Rip Van Winkle by Washington Irving, and other similar stories from around the world.

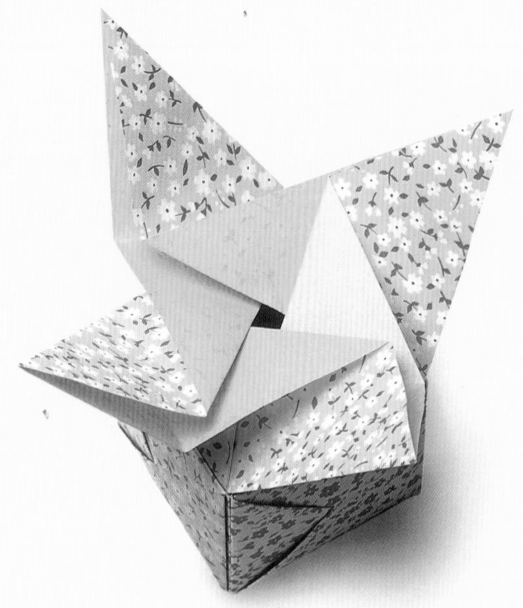

Recently, an origami Tamatebako was discovered in a Japanese book of wood engravings from the year 1734 (shown in the figure below in yellow).

Unfortunately, neither the creator of this masterpiece nor the original folding instructions are known.

Still, the origami historian Masao Okamura arrived at a satisfying reconstruction through his research, comparing numerous traditional works.

I would like to introduce this rediscovered masterpiece on the following pages.

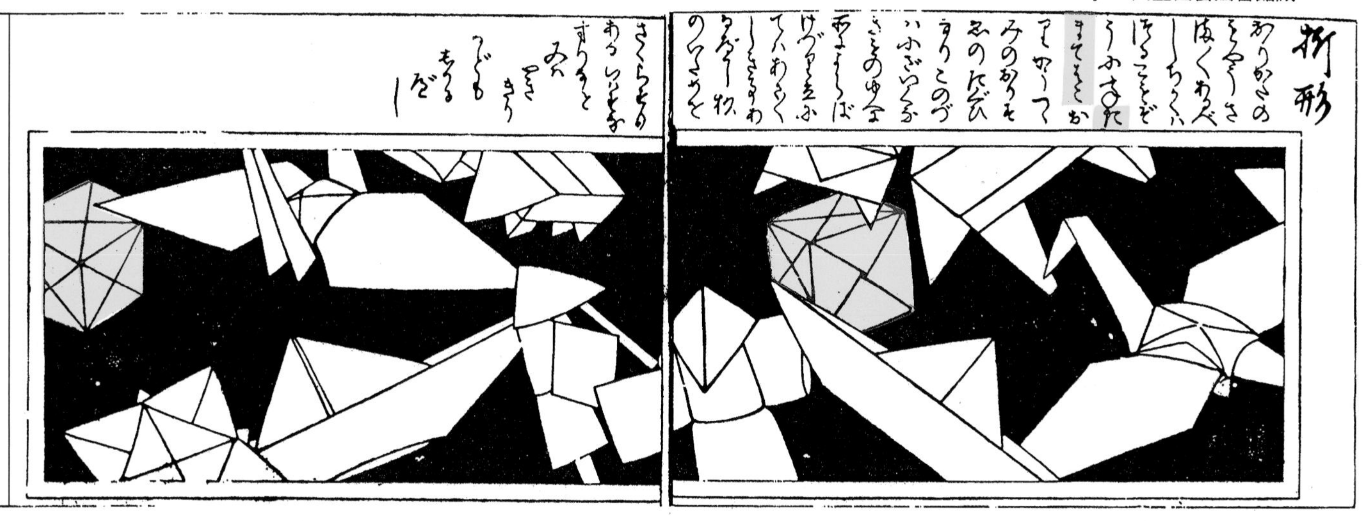

Drawings from the three-volume woodcut book *Ranma-Zushiki (Ranma Sketches)* by Hayato Ohoka, published 1734. The colored origami cube was identified by Yasuo Koyanagi as a Tamatebako, and was published in the 1993 book *Koten-ni-miri-origami* by Satoshi Tagaki.

The Origami Tamatebako

It is possible to open all six sides of the Tamatebako cube. If all six sides are opened at once...

... the cube disappears.

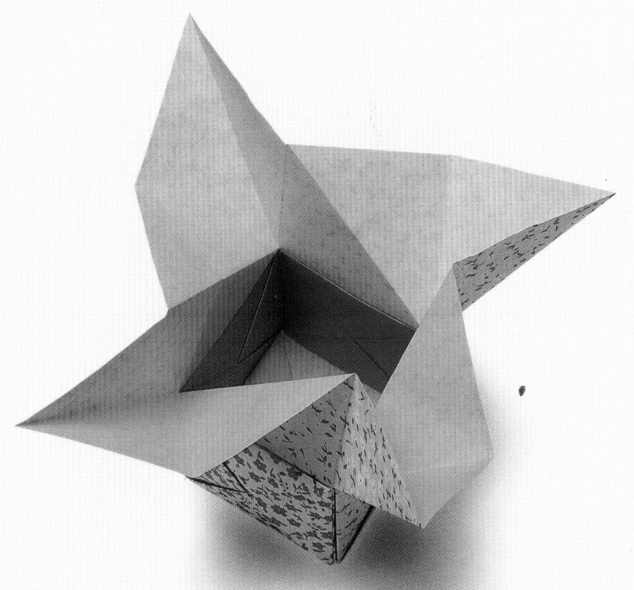

The reconstructed folding instructions are on page 49.

Form and Function

When folding paper, there are two possible goals: to create a new form (metamorphosis of design) or — even more frequently — to wrap something. From the very beginning, origami played a role in this practical function. The functional aspect of folding was recognized long before today's interpretation of origami came into being. (Old terms also indicate the original purpose of the technique.)

If my guess is correct, then the Tamatebako gift box — the name says it all — once served as packaging, similar perhaps to the tatogami. A further example, found by the origami historian Masao Okamura, is the illustration *Tatogami-uri* below, which depicts a tatogami seller. Tatogami (also known as tato) is wrapping made out of folded paper. Today in Japan it is still used as a valuable packaging for kimonos.

According to Okamura, the original picture of the *Tatogami-uri* comes from the period Meio 9 (end of the 16th century). This means that origami works were sold as wrapping for more than 400 years. Consequently, it may be assumed that their use as boxes also occurred 260 years ago, which is as long as the Tamatebako is known to have existed.

However, what particularly fascinates me about the Tamatebako, besides its practical use, is its form. It is a cube, one of the five Platonic bodies, in which geometric–mathematical principles are clearly conveyed. This figure unites all beginnings and directions that are relevant to origami.

The reconstructed folding instructions of the historic model (see page 49) are an example of unit or modular origami, and illustrate the method of dividing a section into three parts. This technique of model construction from several units, or modules, is discussed further in Chapter 3 (page 53ff).

This is the origami wrapping, the tatogami.

Detail of the picture *Tatogami-uri (Tatogami seller)* from *71 Illustrations of Handicrafts,* printed by Tosa Mitsunobu around the end of the 16th century.

Folding Instructions

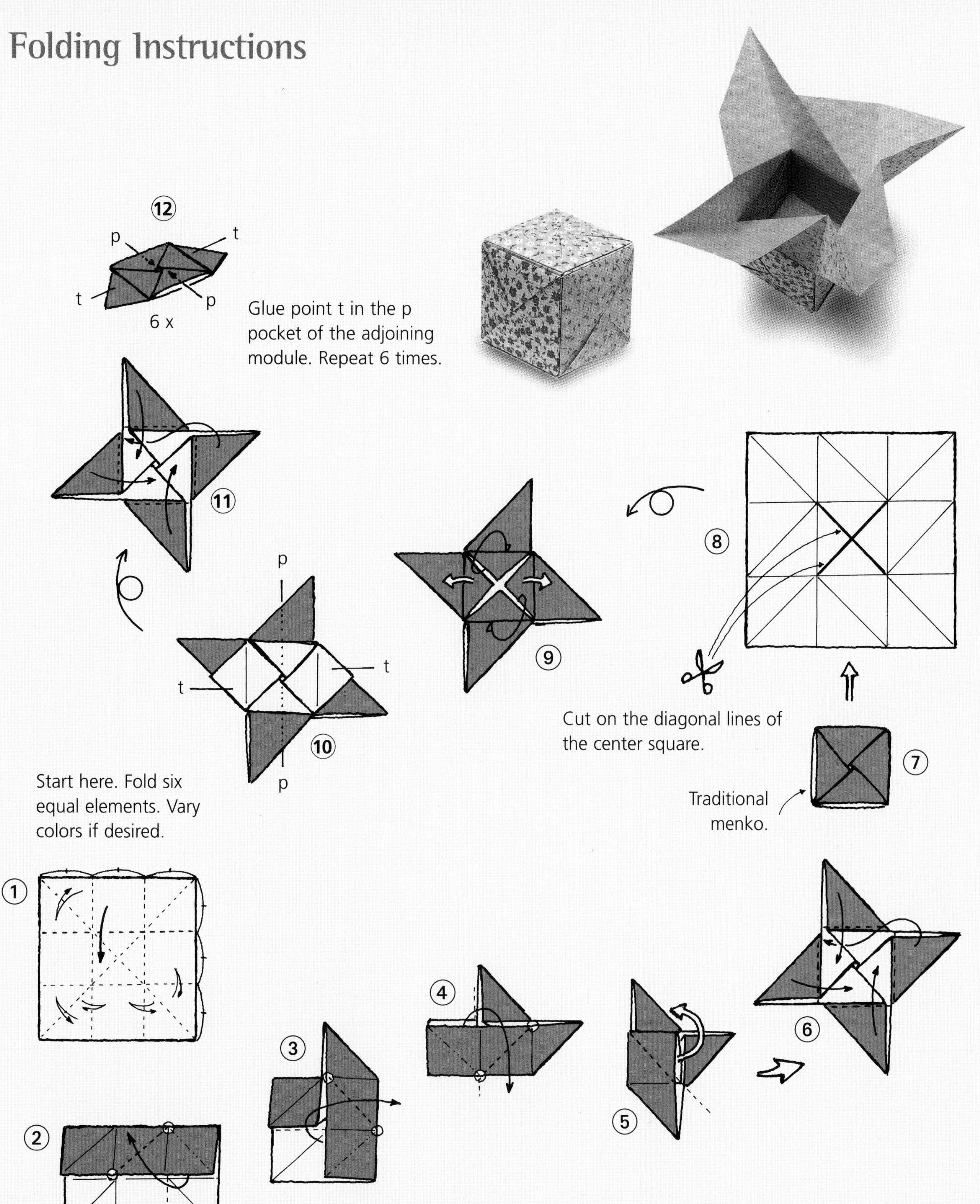

12
p
t
t
p
6 x
Glue point t in the p pocket of the adjoining module. Repeat 6 times.
11
p
t
t
10
p
9
8
Cut on the diagonal lines of the center square.
7
Traditional menko.
Start here. Fold six equal elements. Vary colors if desired.
1
2
3
4
5
6

The Poetry of Fold Lines of a Great Imagiro

In March 1993, I met with the Portuguese artist Paulo Taborda Barreto, who was living in Holland. This man has, in his own way, extended the origami revolution and opened the door to imagination. In his works — all untitled — the viewer can imagine the wind that whispers through the trees, the murmur of a creek, or the ever-changing form of a sand dune. These and other difficult themes found in fine art Barreto calculatedly designed, yet so freely created them that the fold construction is easily visible. Just set your imagination in motion, and listen to your inner self....

In ending this chapter about the new origami, a small part of the unique world of this important imagiro is shown.

The folding technique is not revolutionary, but the imagination with which these three-dimensional pictures are composed is. Also note the deep sense of aesthetics which characterizes the work as a whole.

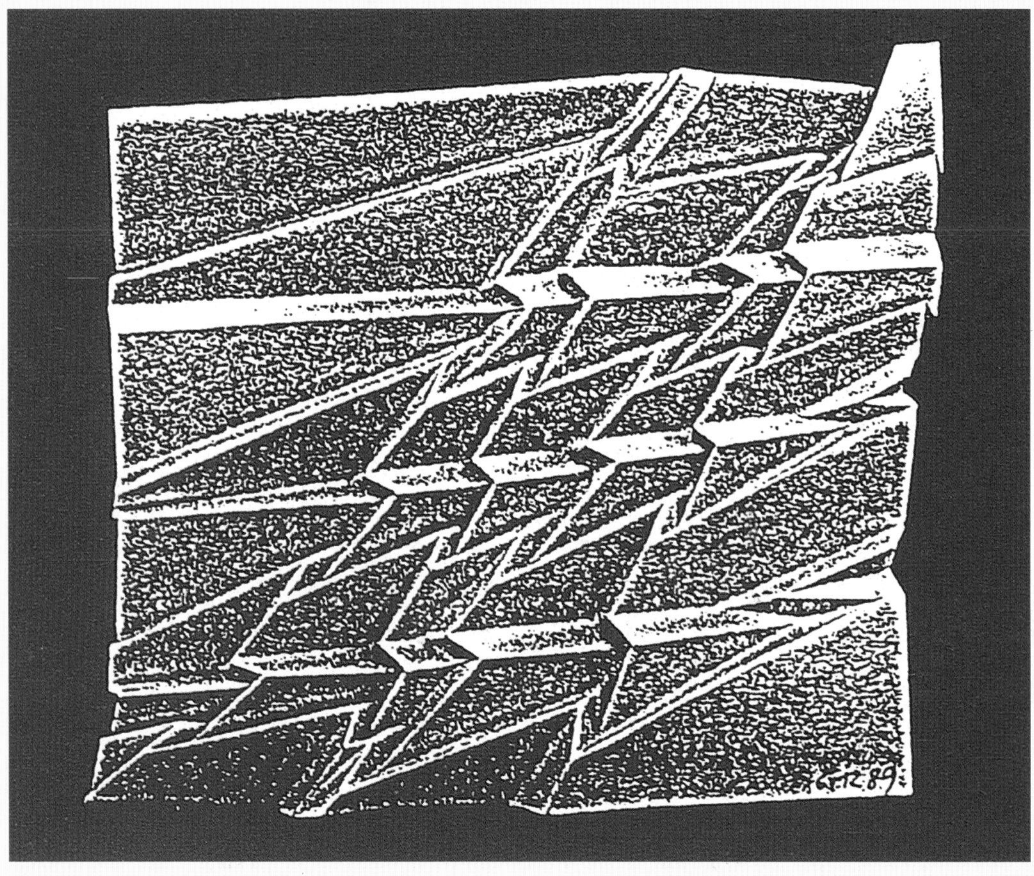

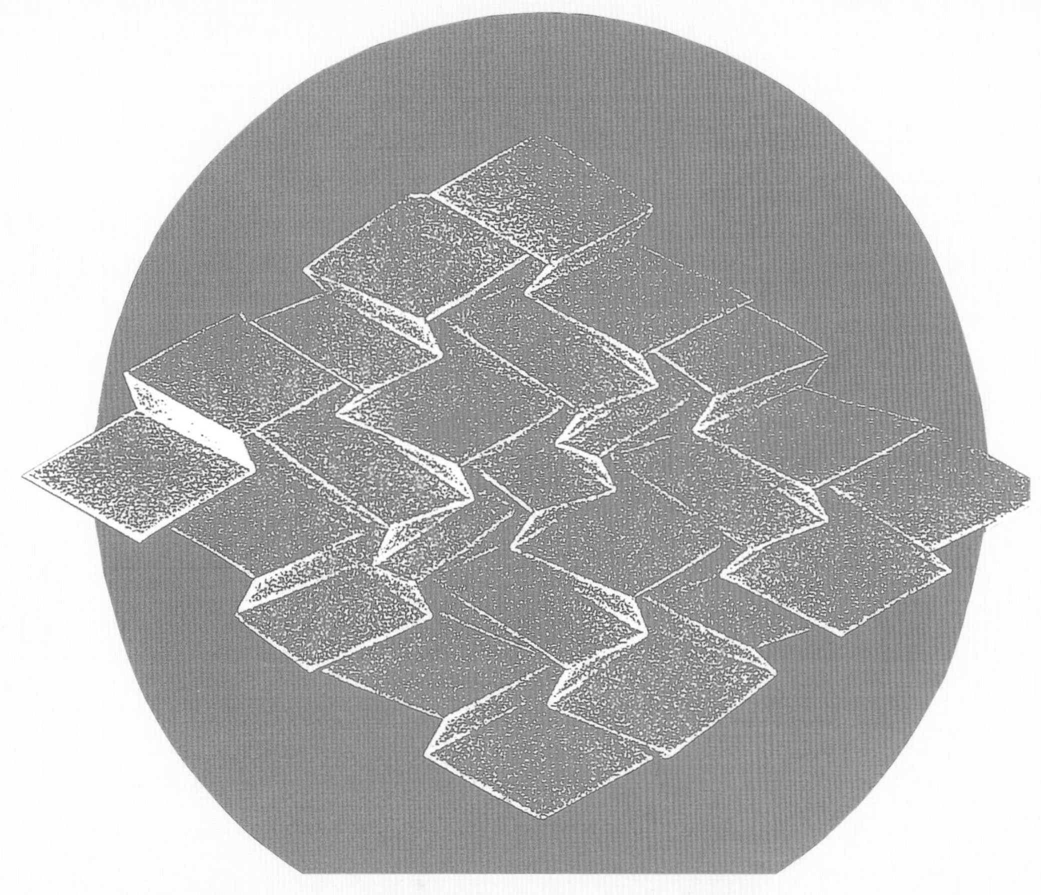

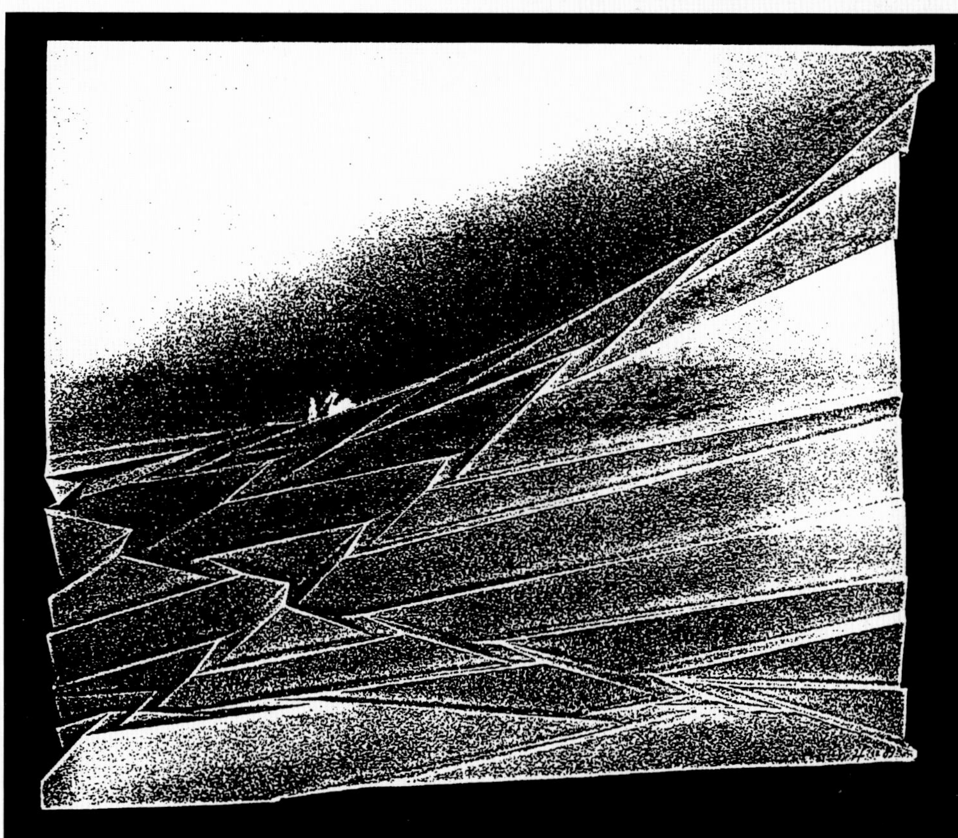

Untitled

by Paulo Taborda Barreto

A uniquely fine geometric origami improvisation.

Untitled

by Paulo Taborda Barreto

Chapter 3 Pinwheels and Modular Origami

In this chapter, a story is told in which the Pinwheel plays the leading role. Additional key roles will be held by the Cube and modular origami.

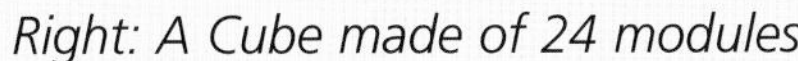

Right: A Cube made of 24 modules

Below: Various Cubes, each made of 6 modules

The Cube: The Fundamental Polyhedron

On page 21, you met the five regular polyhedrons: Tetrahedron, Cube, Octahedron, Dodecahedron, and Icosahedron. They are the basic forms for other geometric polyhedrons (polyhedron means "many surfaced object"). The cube is the fundamental form of all basic forms. It is a familiar figure, yet it is also packed with mystery.

The cube was the base shape for the 260-year-old origami masterpiece, the Tamatebako (see page 46ff). Its transformation is based on a folding technique in which identical single elements (modules) are put together to create an overall form. This rediscovered skill is called modular origami.

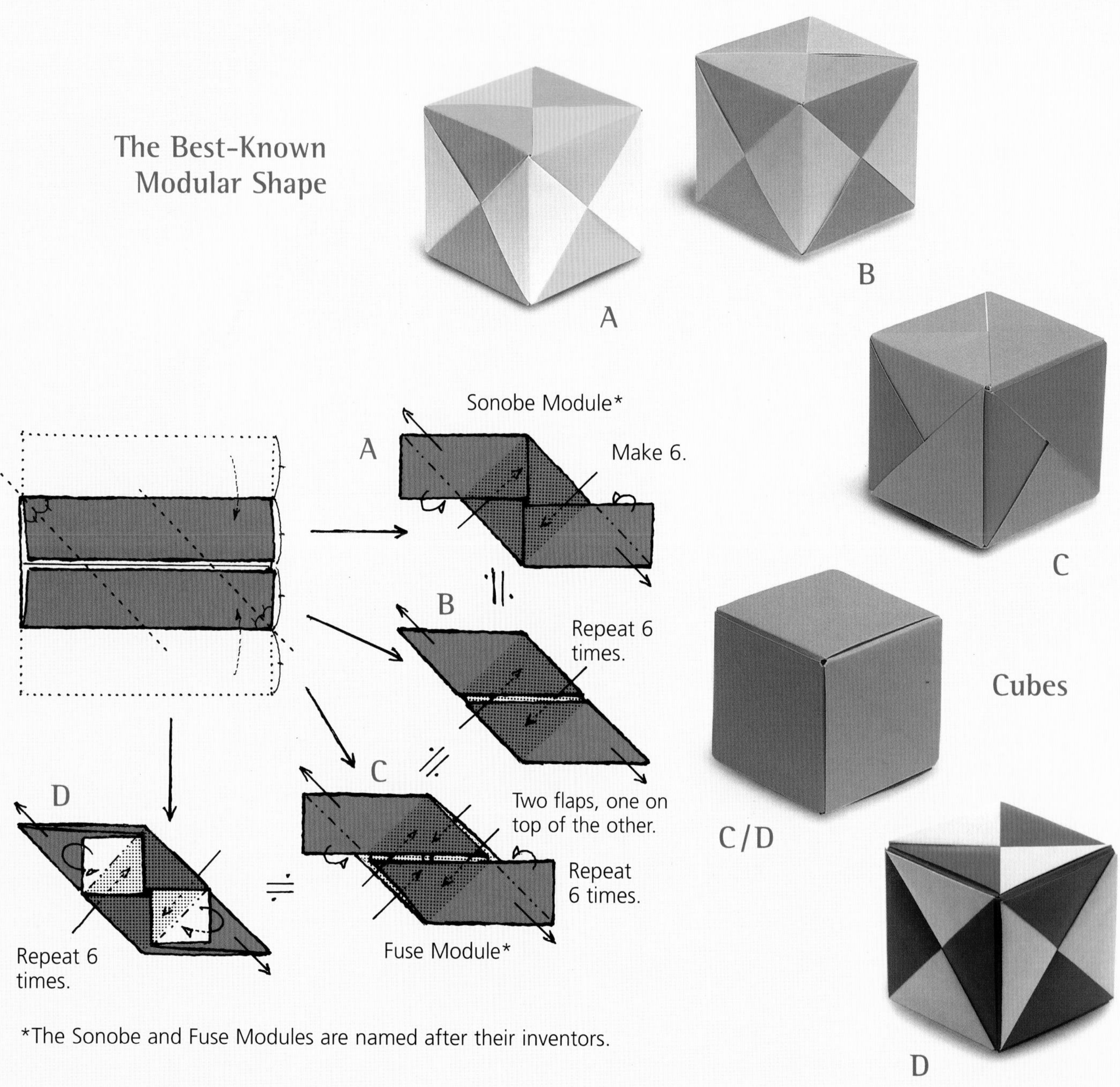

*The Sonobe and Fuse Modules are named after their inventors.

Tamatebako and Pinwheel–Cube Modules

The reconstruction of the historic Tamatebako by Masao Okamura (for folding instructions, see page 49) simultaneously broke origami taboos against using more than one paper and against cutting and gluing. These days, due to the amazing development and expansion of folding techniques, the restrictions on these methods have been dispensed with, allowing the classical conception of origami to grow.

Further development of folding techniques does not mean the simultaneous development of origami. Free yourself from such restrictions by introducing new techniques and concepts into your designs! Only in this way is it possible to create, appreciate, and enjoy historic works like the Tamatebako.

Comparison of Different Modular Cubes

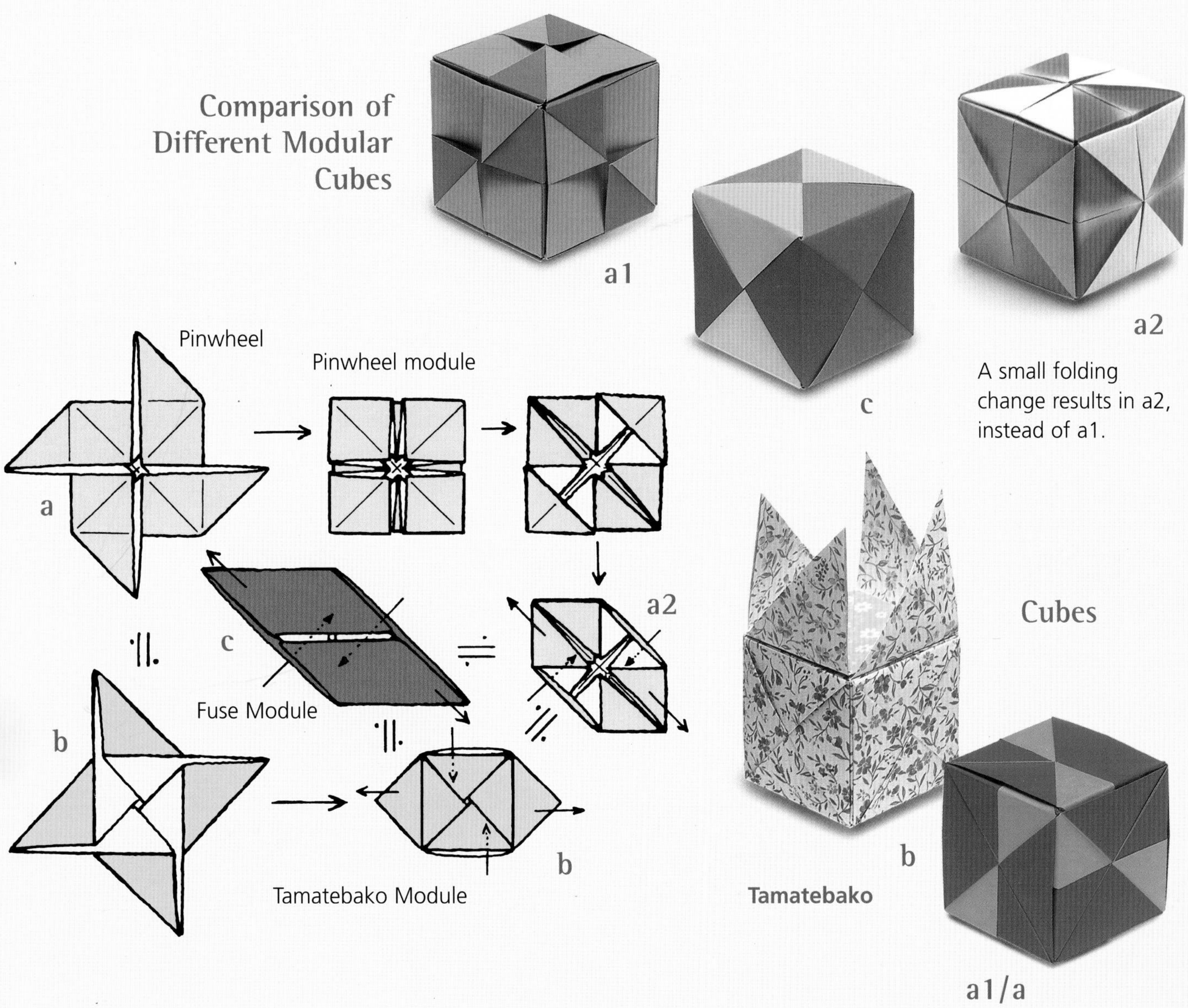

A small folding change results in a2, instead of a1.

The Pinwheel and Its Best Friends

You have certainly seen pinwheels before. Do you know how they are folded? If not, then try following the simple instructions below. The finished paper wheel (Drawing A) then must be made to function. For this you need a thin wooden stick, two matching beads, and a pin (Drawing B).

Is this too much work? Then lay the Pinwheel on a flat surface, bend the wings up, and blow into it from above (Drawing C, page 57). If you change the orientation of the wings, the wheel will spin in the opposite direction.

Now look at Drawing D on page 57. This folded model is known as La Pajarita (Little Bird), but this name is not standard. In Japan this figure is called Little Dog, in Germany it is the Rooster.... Each country, each person sees something different....

Finally, consider illustration E on page 57; something will surely strike you.... All these models are variations of the Pinwheel and, so to speak, its best friends. If you can fold these figures, you already have intermediate level knowledge of origami.

Pinwheel

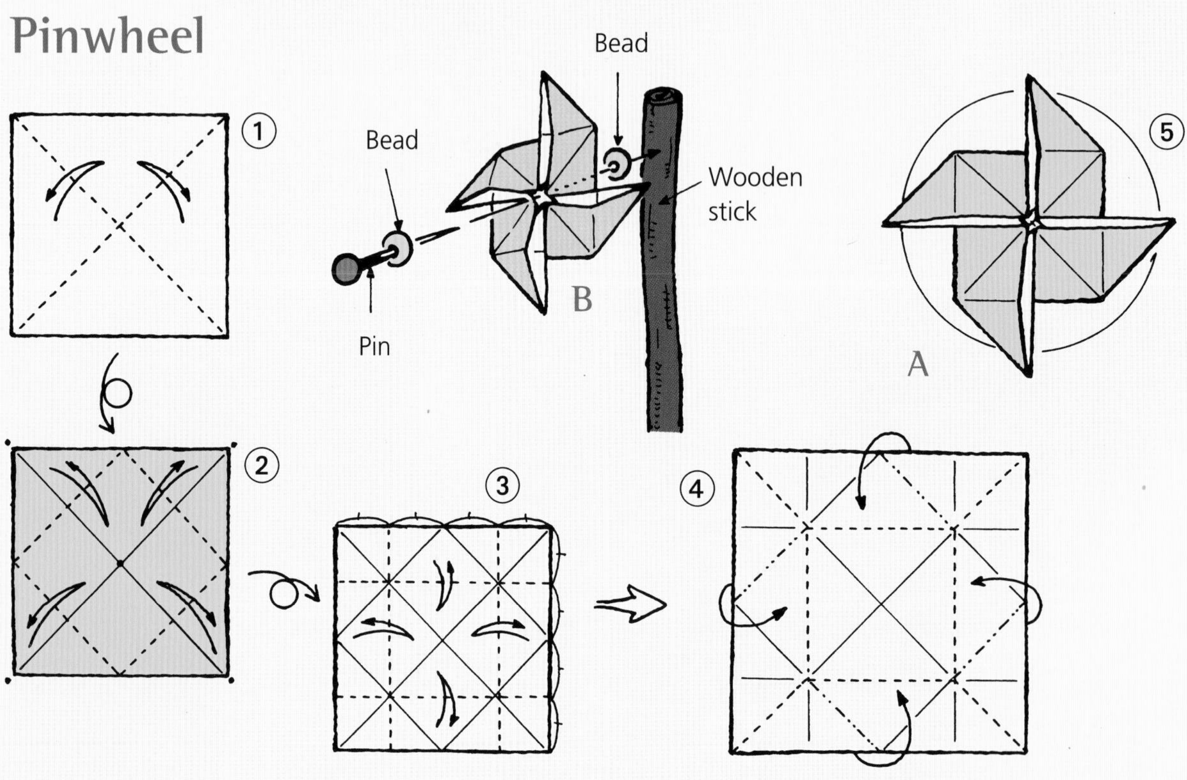

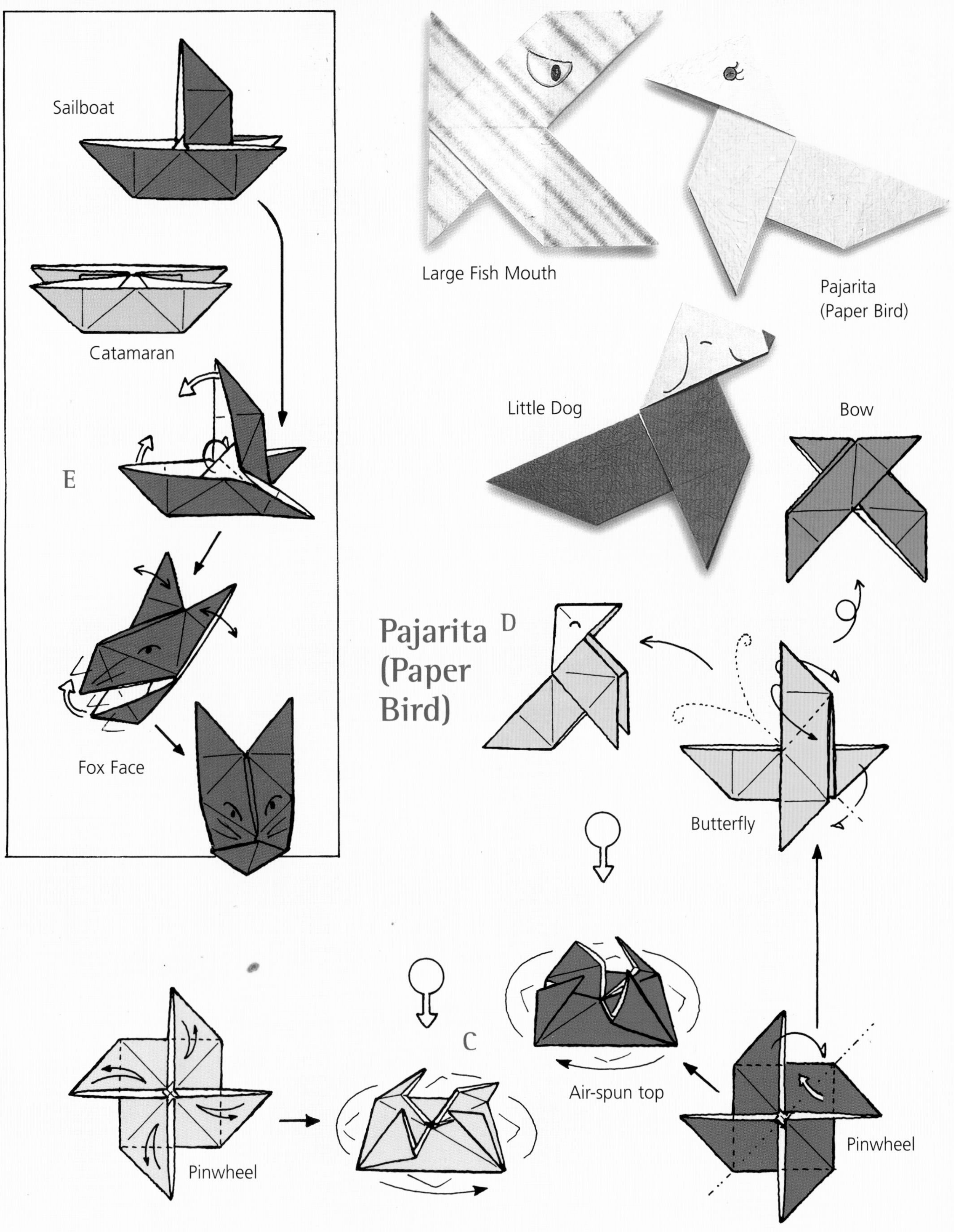
Sailboat
Catamaran
E
Fox Face
Large Fish Mouth
Pajarita
(Paper Bird)
Little Dog
Bow
Pajarita
(Paper
Bird)
D
Butterfly
C
Air-spun top
Pinwheel
Pinwheel

Variations on the Pinwheel

Now fold another Pinwheel base (Drawing A below); then pull up the four wing flaps and squash flat. From the new form (Drawing B), many other Pinwheels can be constructed.

Variation C is especially interesting: if you fold all four of its corners towards the back (Drawing D), a perfect octagon emerges.

Furthermore, C is an example of one of the basic forms mentioned by the German teacher Froebel (see page 18). From this and from its association with the Cube, it is possible to develop ideas which, in turn, expand the meaning of modular origami. Read more about this subject on the following pages.

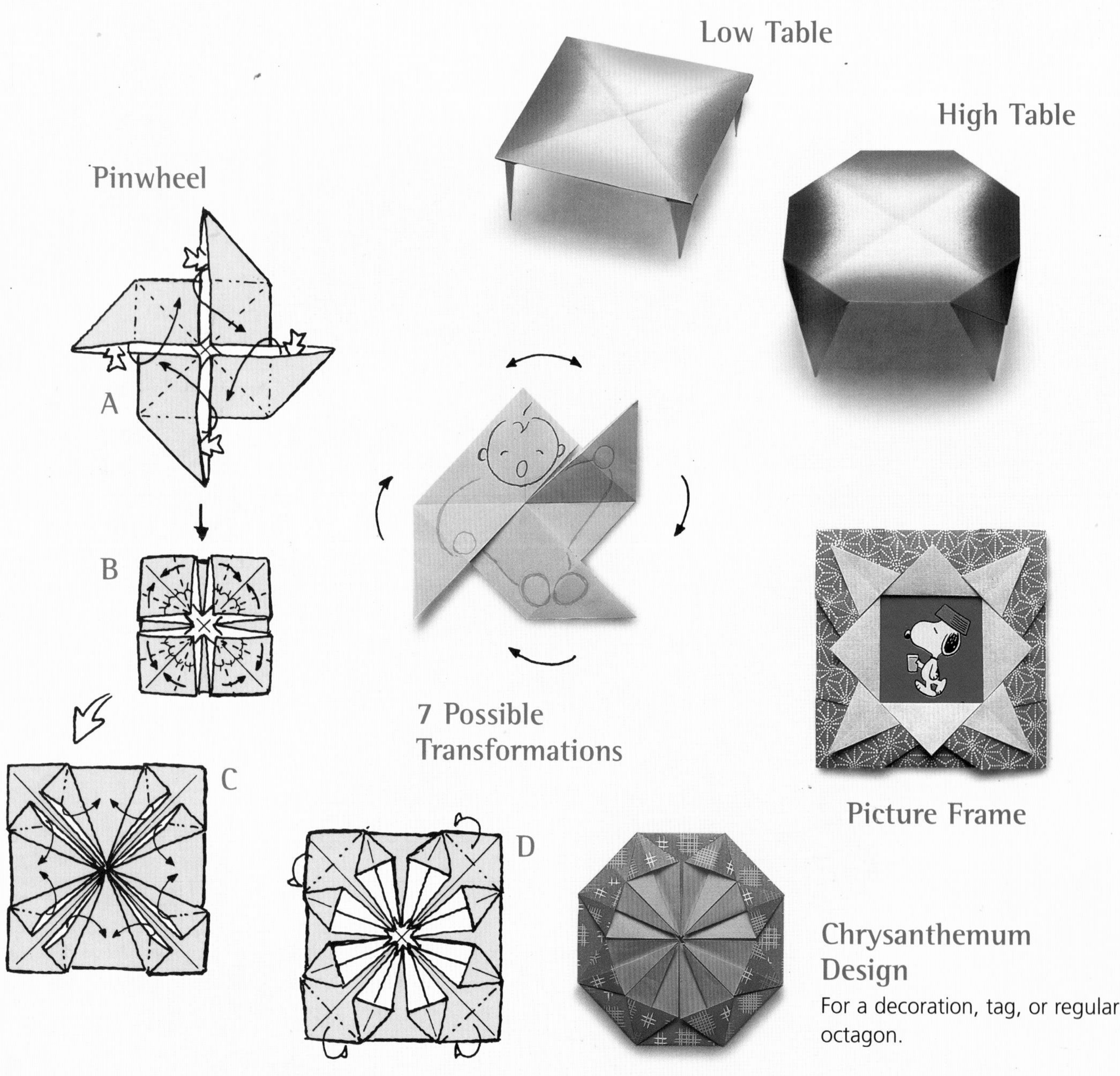

Low Table

High Table

7 Possible Transformations

Picture Frame

Chrysanthemum Design

For a decoration, tag, or regular octagon.

Froebel's Basic Forms

Here you see a small selection of patterns based on the principles of Froebel's basic forms. I have chosen original Froebel patterns that complement the Pinwheel theme, and I added some of my own.

The number of different possibilities is astronomical. The same is true for other paper forms.

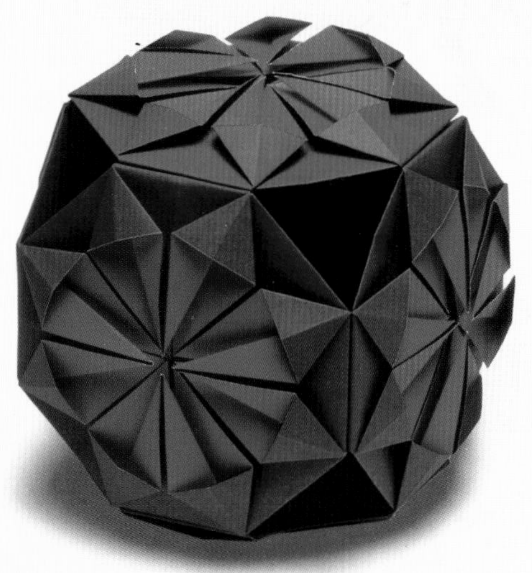

This decorative polyhedron consists of six individual octagonal elements (Form D, page 58) which are glued together at the flaps. The shape is basically a variation of the Cube, the regular octagons of Basic Form D forming the Cube module.

Froebel's Basic Forms as Cube Modules

Froebel's basic forms arrived in Japan along with his kindergarten concept during the Meiji period (1868 to 1912), where they were known as *birei-shiki* (display fold system). When I first became acquainted with them they were known as *moyou-ori* (pattern folds), and to be honest, I was not especially impressed with them. But after I discovered the intricate connection between the basic forms and the Cube, they took on a new appeal. More than half of the forms can be used as modules to build a Cube without any problem. They have another interesting feature, which is that the points of attachment do not have to be glued.

But the technical–aesthetic results, the joy of invention, and the discovery of new patterns possible with these basic forms are even more important. In this way, Froebel's system of pattern folds offers a multitude of creative possibilities for the origami beginner as well.

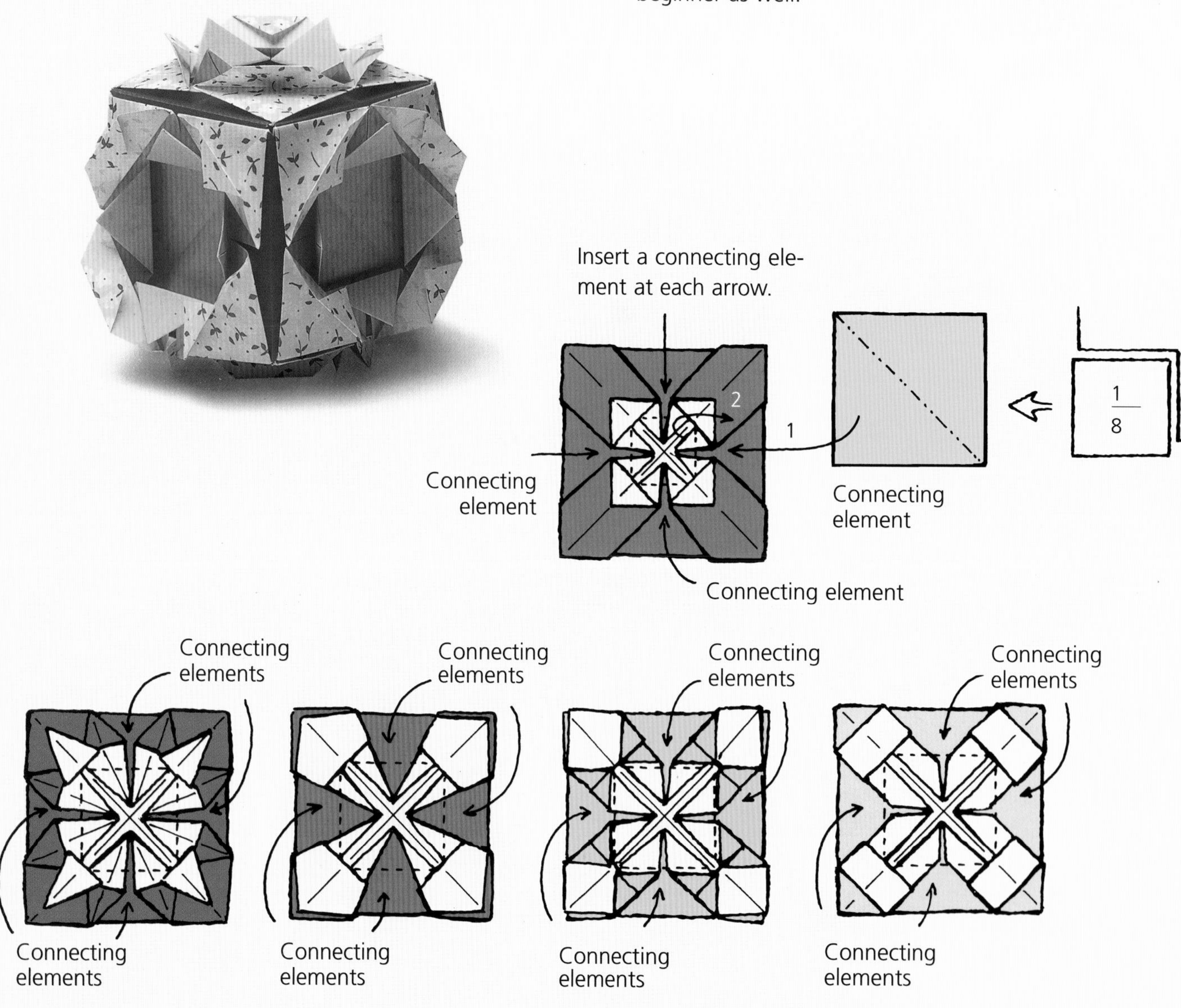

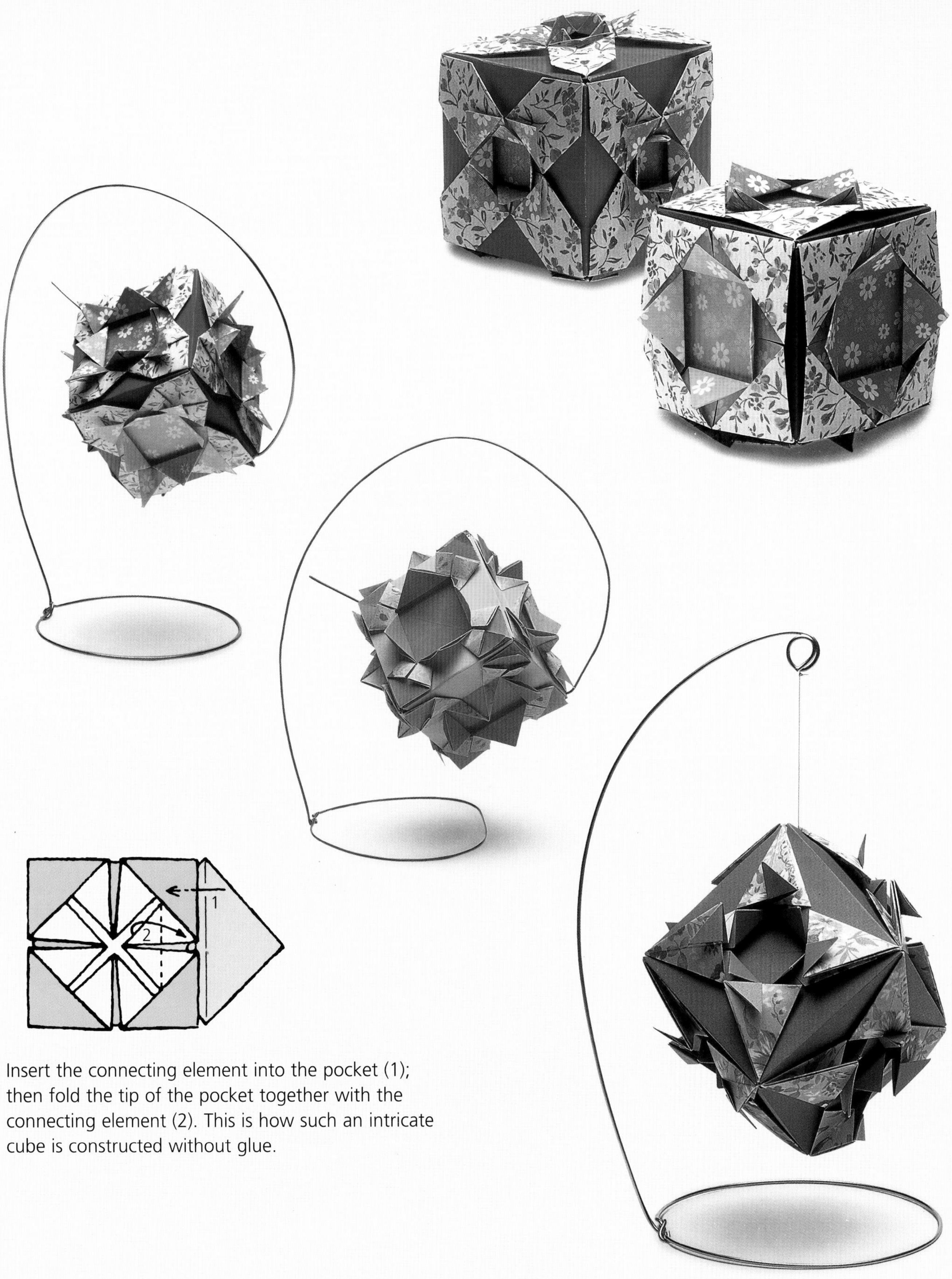

Insert the connecting element into the pocket (1); then fold the tip of the pocket together with the connecting element (2). This is how such an intricate cube is constructed without glue.

The Wheel of Ideas Spins Further

The Tamatebako module (Drawing B below and page 55), in which squares are divided into three parts, can be reinterpreted as a variation of the Pinwheel (Drawing A) if simply divided into four parts. If this idea is taken further, additional variants of Pinwheels are possible, as a result of the change in the proportions of the sections.

As with varying patterns starting from a basic form (see pages 59 to 61), altering the proportions of a section leads to new and interesting modules.

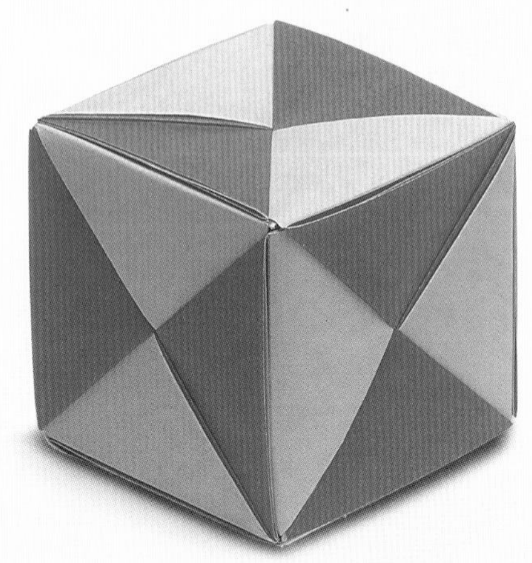

Variations by Changing the Number of Sections

Three sections

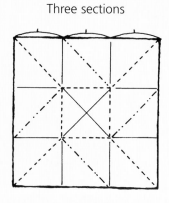

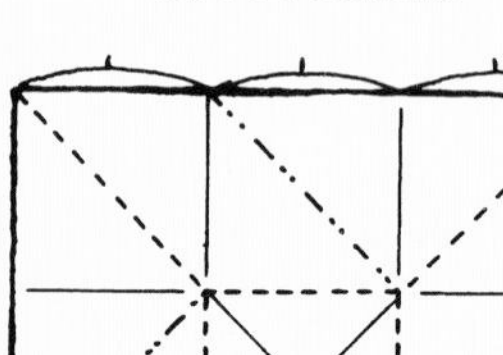

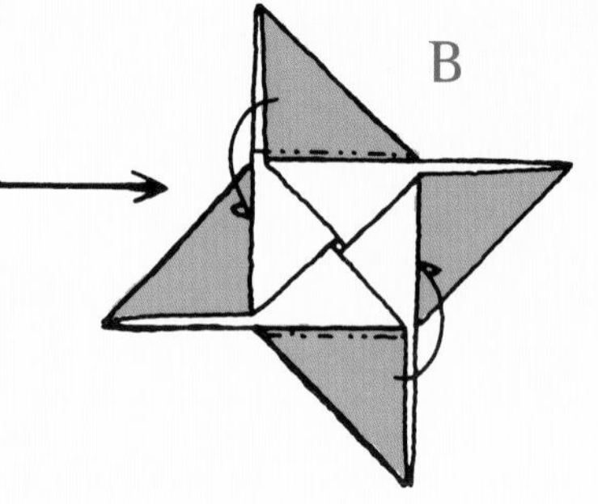

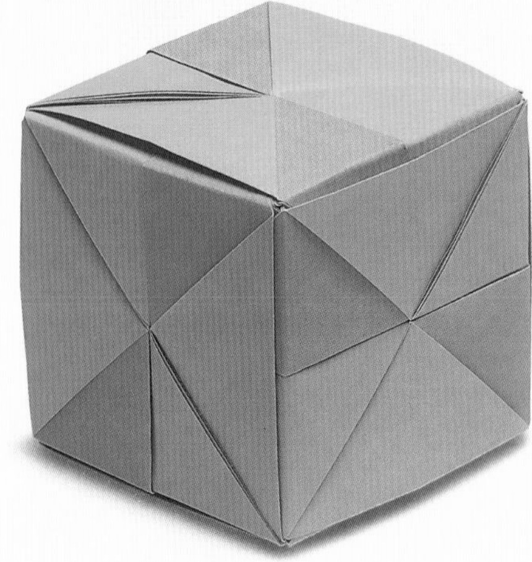

Make 6.

Four sections

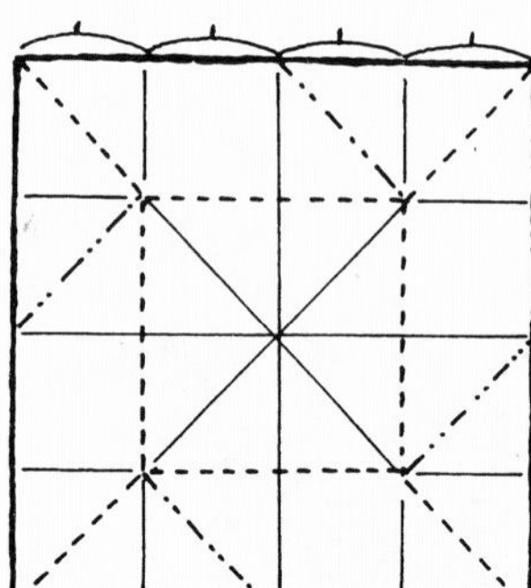

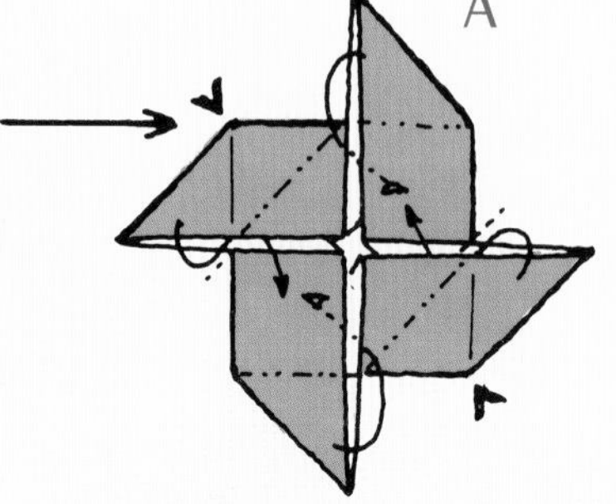

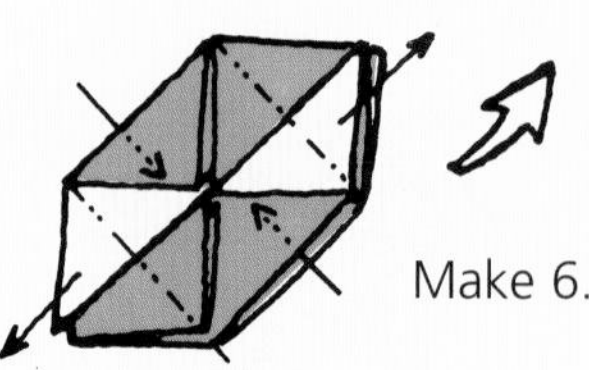

Make 6.

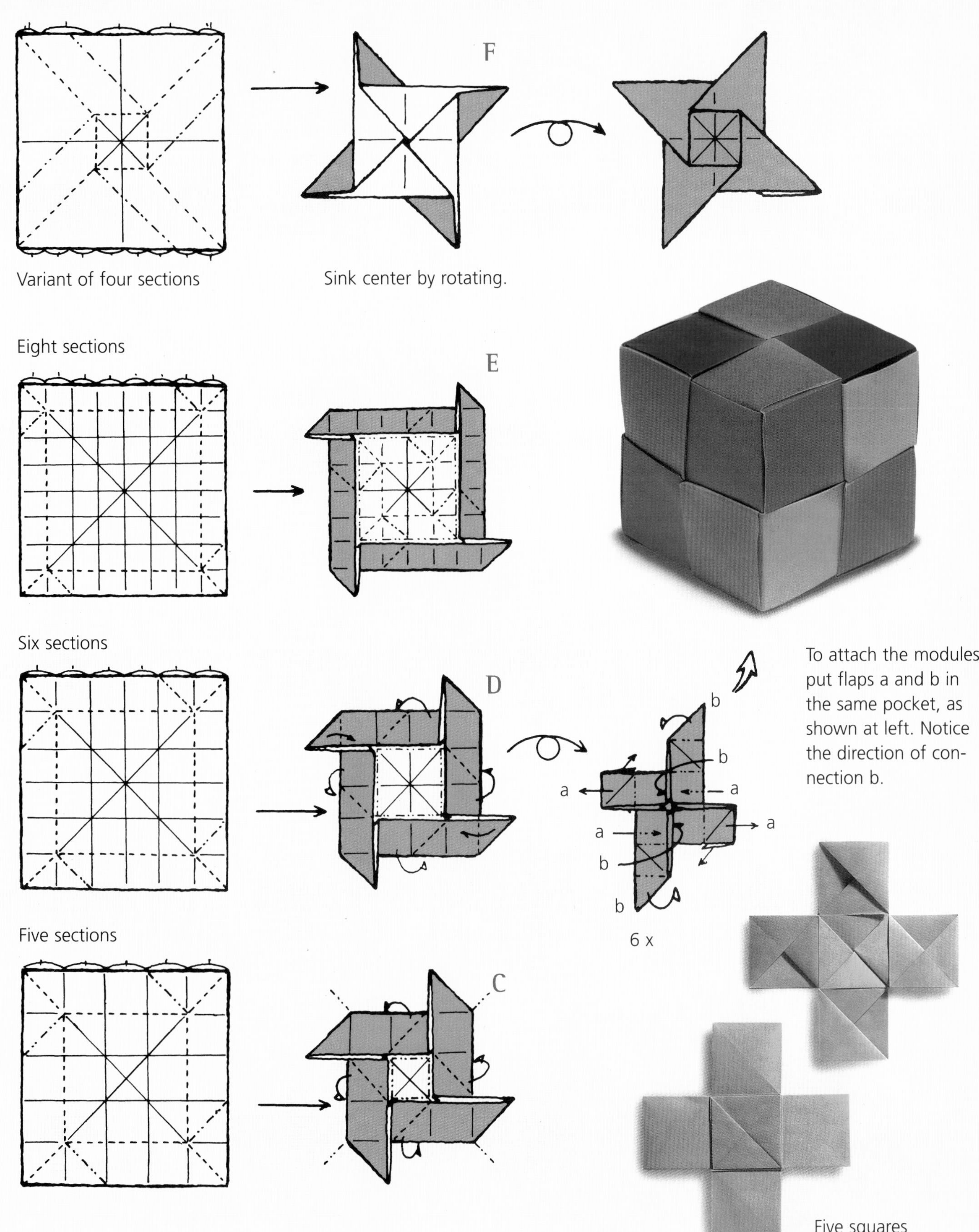

Variant of four sections

Sink center by rotating.

Eight sections

Six sections

Five sections

To attach the modules, put flaps a and b in the same pocket, as shown at left. Notice the direction of connection b.

Five squares

New Pinwheel Snowflakes

In Chapter 2 (see pages 42 to 45), I introduced Snowflakes made by Professor Suzuki. Now look again at Froebel's Basic Forms on page 59. Perhaps you feel that some of these patterns remind you of snowflakes? That is exactly what happened to me. Some of my designs based on perfect hexagons can be seen on page 65.

Use the creative methods of shape association (page 38) and the Pinwheel variation techniques (page 58) we have shown. This page intentionally shows only two basic patterns, I and II; your imagination and ingenuity will lead you to your own brilliant designs. Have fun!

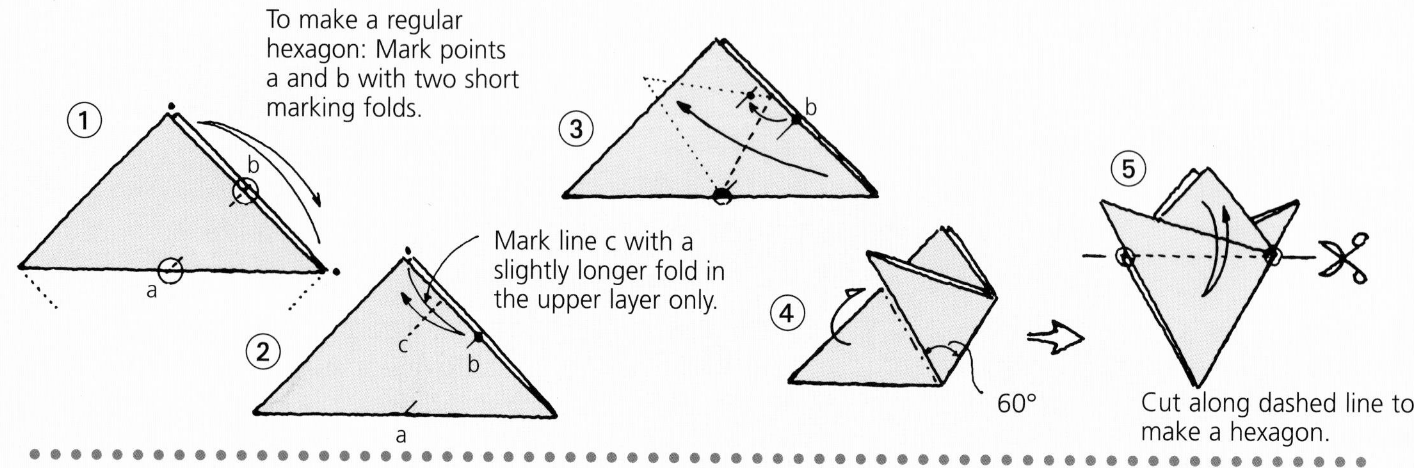

1
To make a regular hexagon: Mark points a and b with two short marking folds.
b
a
2
Mark line c with a slightly longer fold in the upper layer only.
c
b
a
3
b
4
60°
5
Cut along dashed line to make a hexagon.

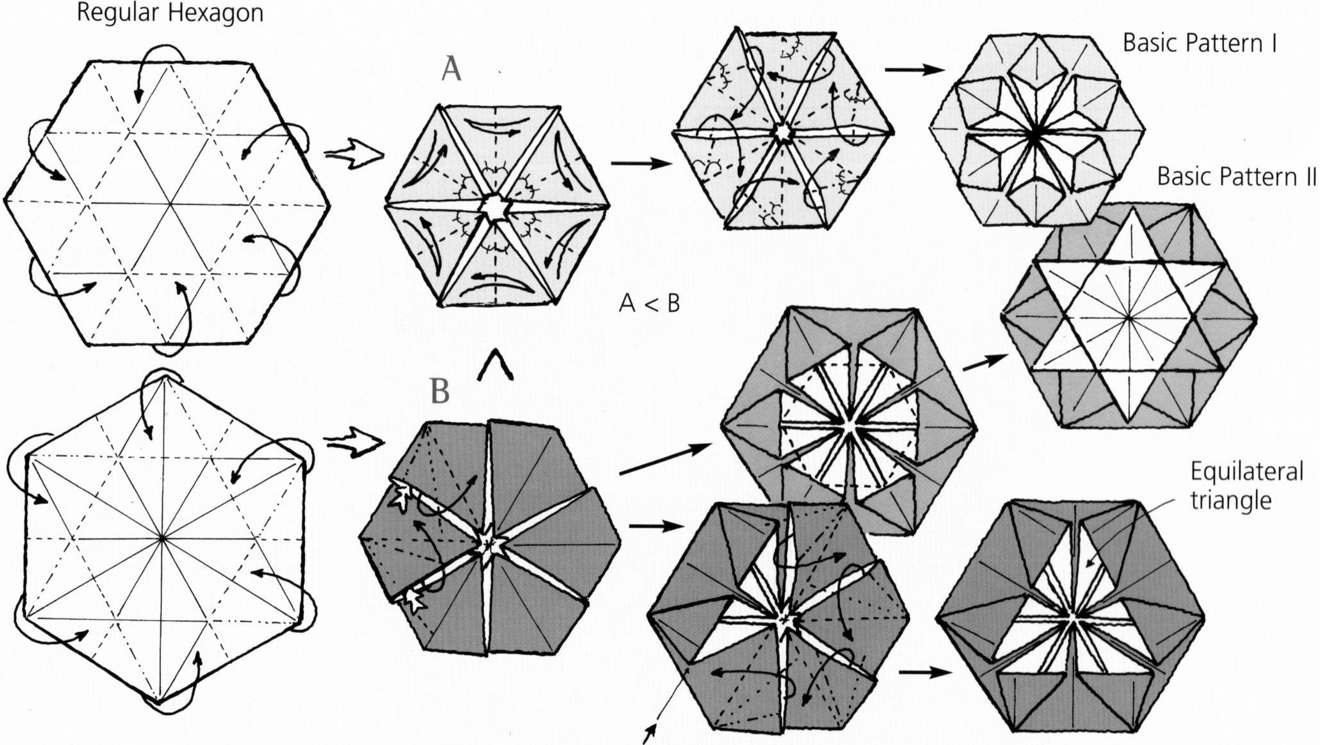

The inside edges become straight lines parallel to the folded hexagon's edge.

Type I and II Pinwheel–Cube Modules

Have you realized that the Pinwheel and Froebel's Basic Forms are based on the same principles? If a large part of Froebel's forms can serve as Cube modules (see page 59), isn't it also possible that the Pinwheel module might be used for the same purpose?

In order to answer this question, I have searched for solutions with the aid of connecting pockets and joining elements — as we did with the basic forms on page 60/61 — in order to attach Pinwheel modules. Three solutions are shown here.

Each has specific attributes, but the most possibilities for expansion and development are offered by the Type III modules, which I have called Super Pinwheel Modules (see page 67). You will find forms derived from Type III on pages 68 to 71. The photos on page 67 show cubes based on modules of Types I and II.

However, this is only a small part of all possible variations. Discover your own patterns by letting your imagination run rampant!

Pinwheel

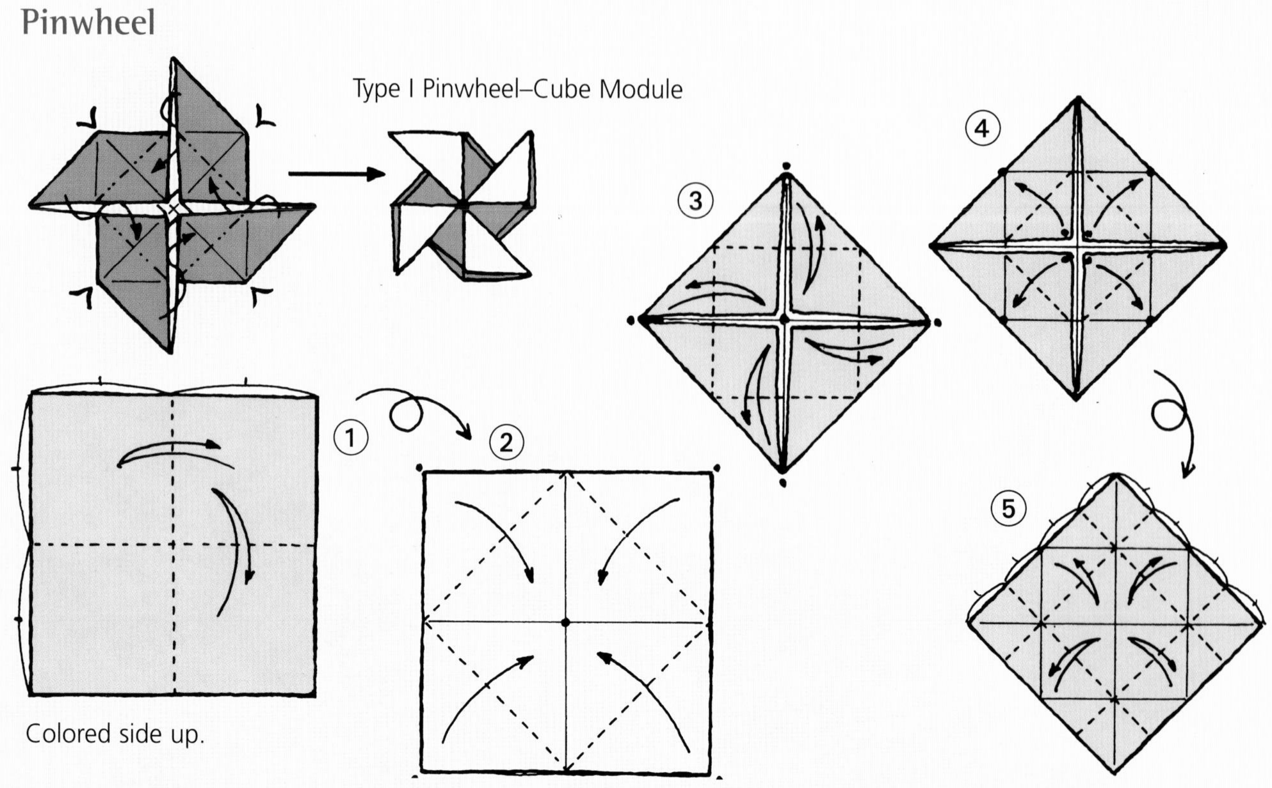

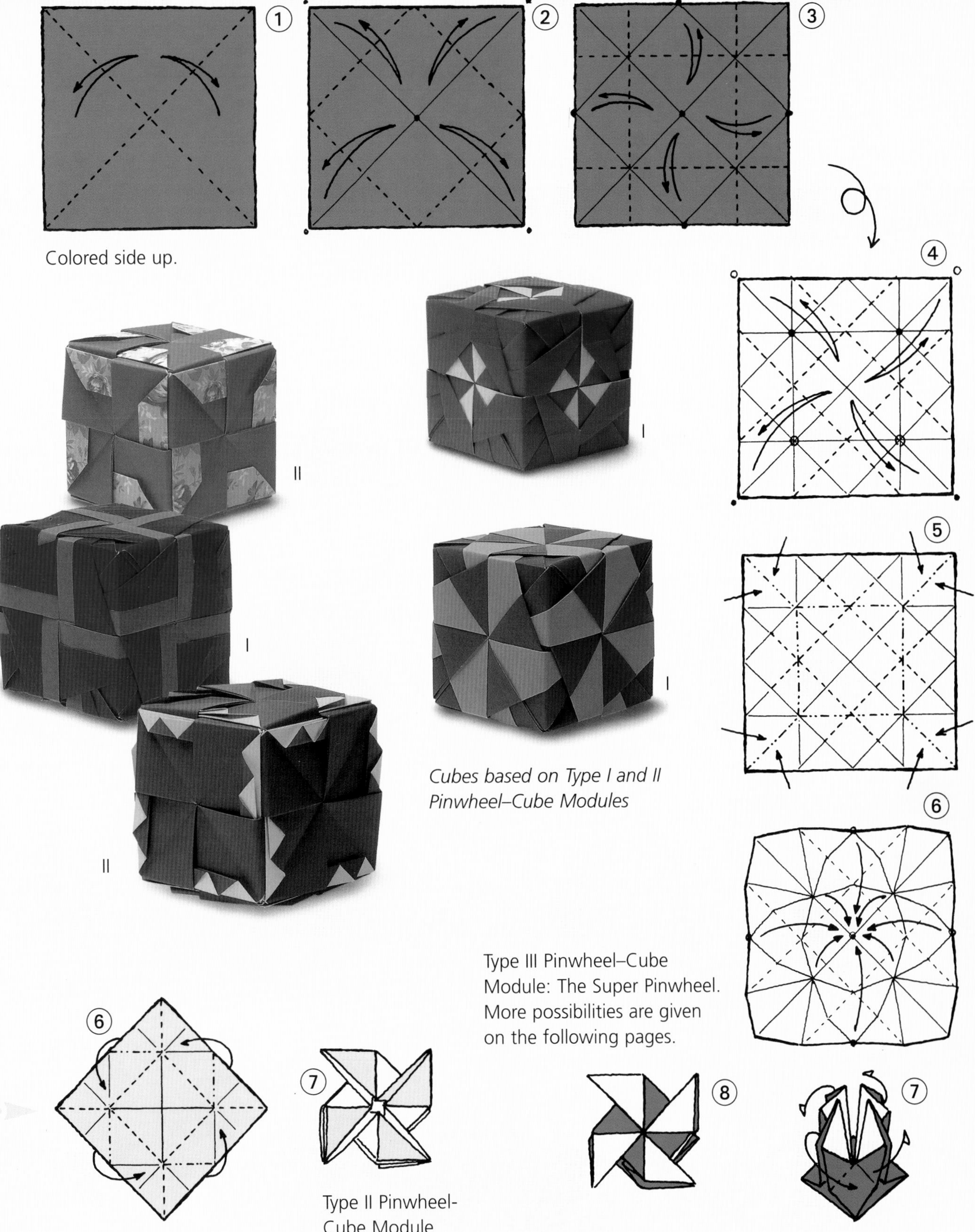

Cubes based on Type I and II Pinwheel–Cube Modules

Type III Pinwheel–Cube Module: The Super Pinwheel. More possibilities are given on the following pages.

Type II Pinwheel-Cube Module

Type III Super Pinwheel–Cube Modules

On page 60 you saw how cubes can be constructed from many of Froebel's basic forms with help from connecting elements and without the need for gluing. In a very similar way, with the Super Pinwheel modules, all of Froebel's basic forms can also be put together in cubes, but here the attachment pieces basically must be glued together.

This may seem to be a technical step backwards, but the supposed disadvantage has, besides the larger pattern variation, something else to offer: the cube can be opened and spread out. An example of this new design possibility and its quality can be seen on page 69 (the Panorama Box).

Type III Super Pinwheel–Cube Module

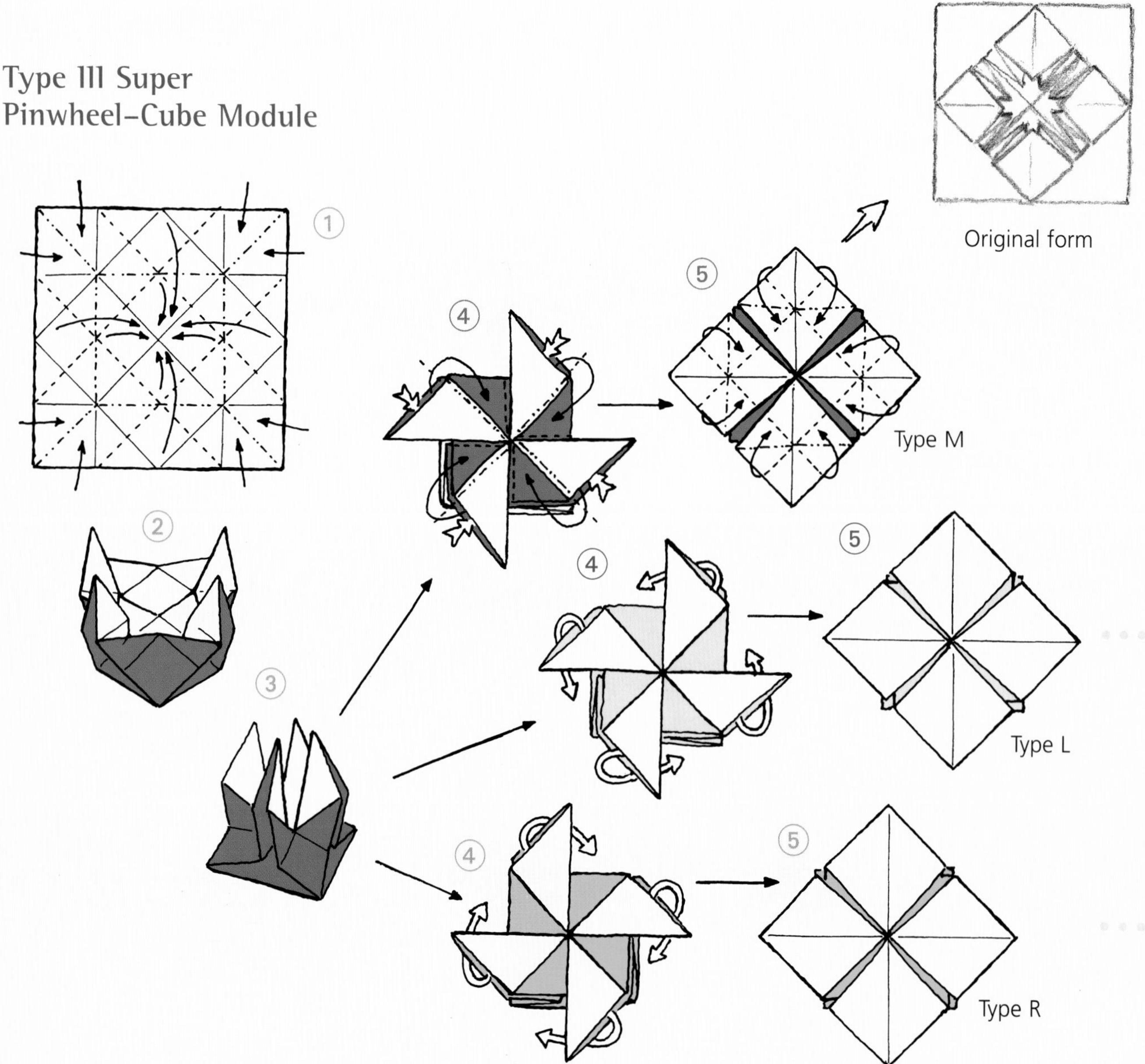

Panorama Box

It is possible to create a Panorama by unfolding and spreading out a cube and then gluing small origami models onto the surface. For example, a landscape or the ocean can be easily portrayed. Be careful to firmly attach the concealed flaps together and place the Panorama elements so they do not prevent the cube from closing. The folding instructions for the Sailboat and the Whale can be found on pages 27 and 38.

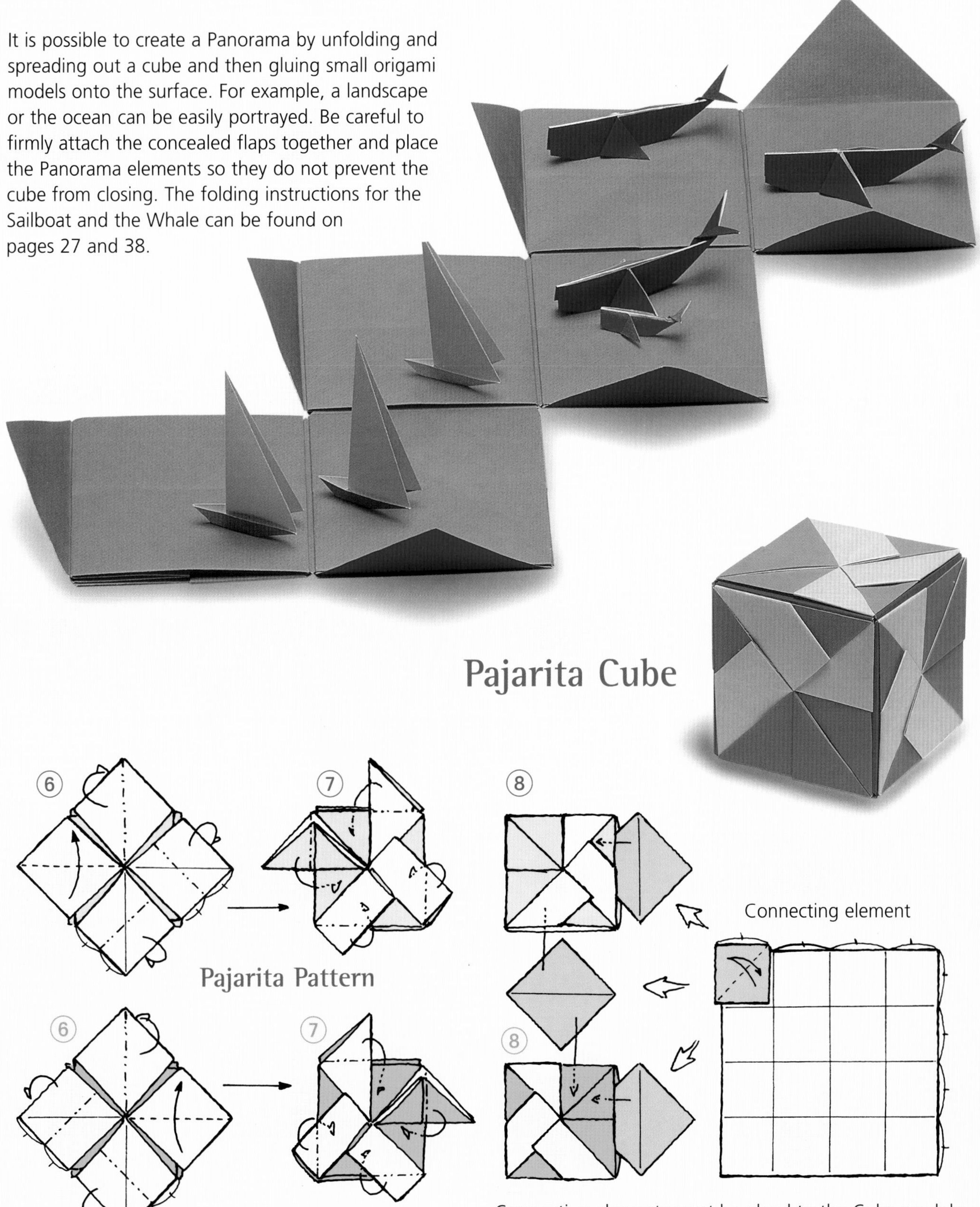

Connecting elements must be glued to the Cube module.

Crane Cubes

An additional Cube module developed from the Super Pinwheel is the Orizuru (Crane) Pattern. Try to develop your own patterns — the possibilities are endless.

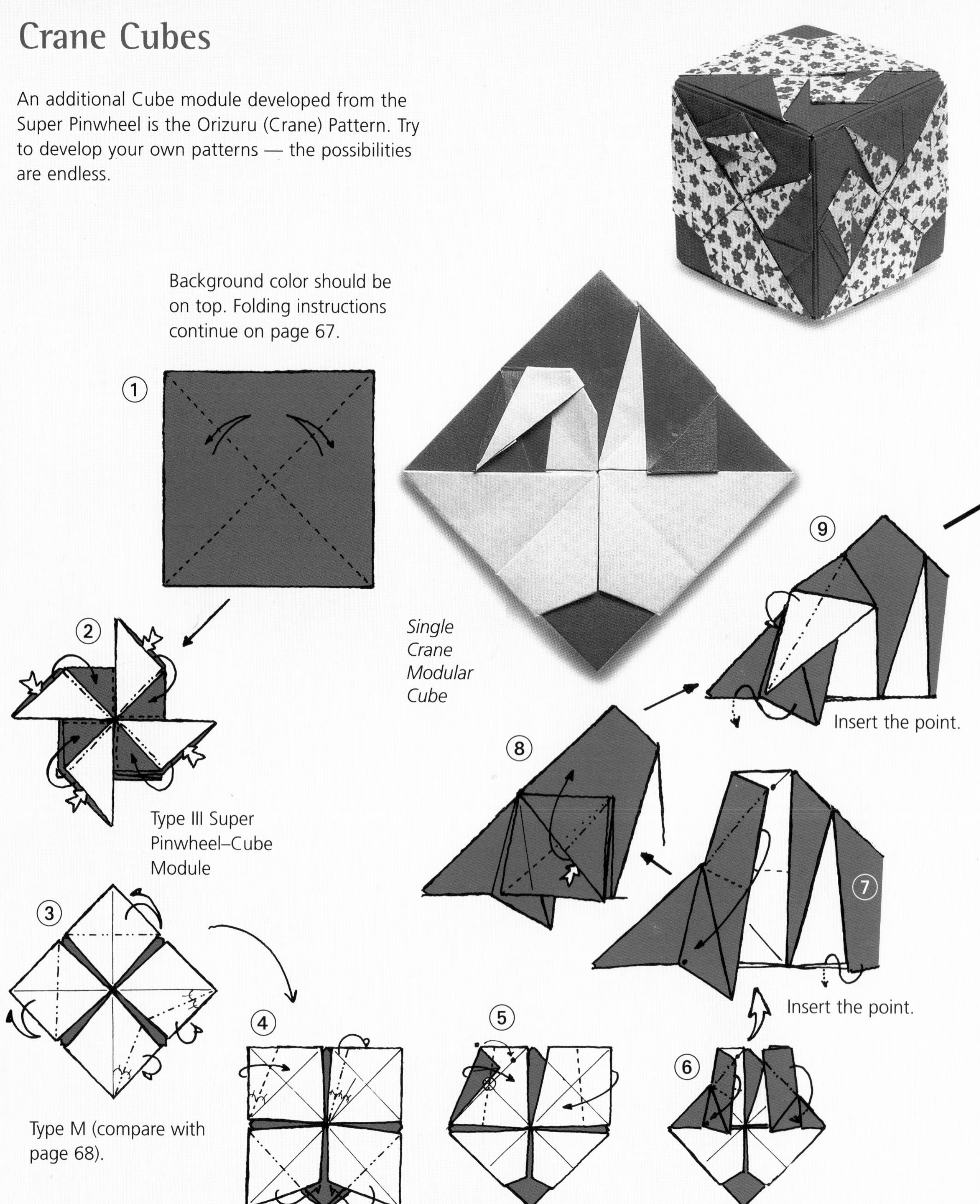

Background color should be on top. Folding instructions continue on page 67.
①
②
Type III Super Pinwheel–Cube Module
③
Type M (compare with page 68).
④
⑤
⑥
⑦
Insert the point.
⑧
⑨
Insert the point.

Single Crane Modular Cube

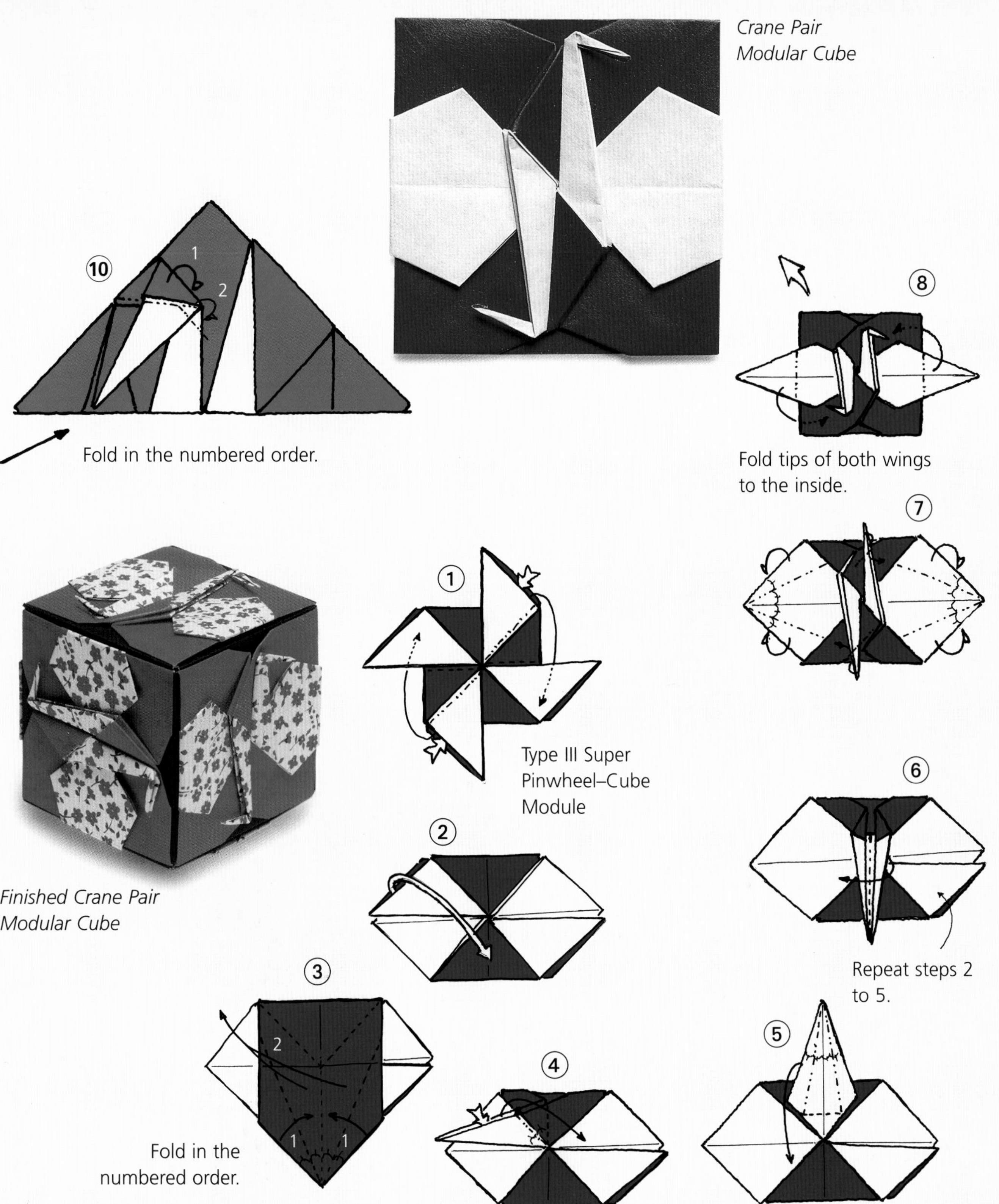

10
1
2
Fold in the numbered order.
8
Fold tips of both wings to the inside.
7
1
Type III Super Pinwheel–Cube Module
2
6
Repeat steps 2 to 5.
3
2
1
1
Fold in the numbered order.
4
5

Crane Pair Modular Cube

Finished Crane Pair Modular Cube

Index

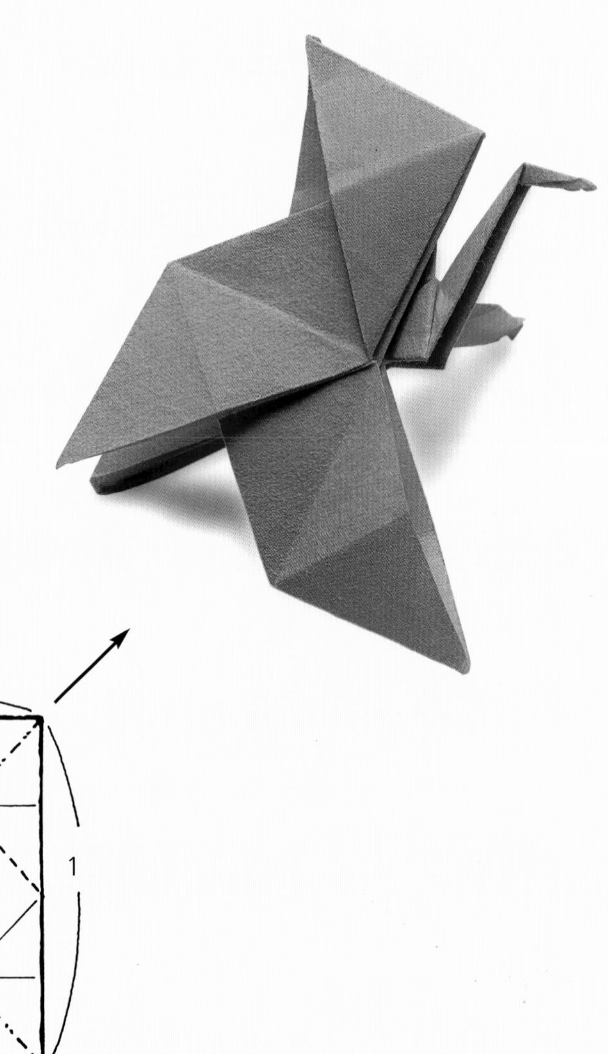

DISCARD
DISCARD